WE MADE THE HEADLINES POSSIBLE

The Critical Contribution of the Rear Echelon in World War II

GEORGE N. HAVENS

First Sergeant, U.S. Army (Ret.)

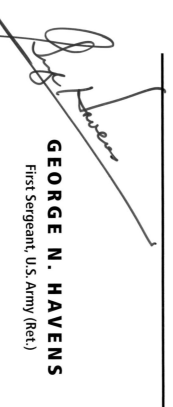

GREENLEAF BOOK GROUP LLC

Cleveland • Chicago • Boca Grande • San Francisco

©2003 George N. Havens

ISBN: 1-929774-15-X

Library of Congress Control Number: 2002110381

Cover design and layout by Francine Smith

Maps by Kurt Roscoe

Submit all requests for reprinting to:
Greenleaf Book Group LLC
660 Elmwood Point, Aurora, OH 44202

Published in the United States by
Greenleaf Book Group LLC, Cleveland, Ohio.

www.greenleafbookgroup.com

Headlines from The Stars and Stripes: Reprinted by permission from
European and Pacific Stars and Stripes, a Department of Defense publication.
©2002 European and Pacific Stars and Stripes

Cover illustration: Copyright ©1945 by The New York Times Co. Reprinted
by permission.

Unfortunately the photographers for photos in this book are not known,
but we acknowledge their work with appreciation.

Dedication

To my GI comrades of
World War II, the citizen soldiers,
for their courage and heroism
in combat and in logistics.

Rationale

Someone has observed that when an individual dies, a lifelong "library" disappears. I wanted to get this portion of my "library" into print while that was still possible.

G.N.H.

Theme

To relate the essential contribution of the
rear-area support soldiers to the Allied victory in
World War II by telling the story of:

One critical location,
the Port of Antwerp, Belgium

One company, the 105th Port Marine
Maintenance Co., Transportation Corps

One individual GI, the author

Contents

*Author's note: Military format is used for dates: day/month/
year and for times: 24-hour designations.*

Maps

The Setting

*World War II was the deadliest conflict
in modern history.*

— Williamson Murray and Allan Millett
A War to be Won

World War II was the last "good war."

— Studs Terkel
The Good War

*World War II… remains the defining event of the
modern era.*

— David M. Kennedy
Freedom from Fear

*The conflict was poised on a knife edge in the middle
years of the war…
The most significant turning-point in…the modern era.*

— Richard Overy
Why the Allies Won

Preface

Direct, personal involvement in a historical event of the ferocity, uniqueness, and scope of World War II etches a deep, indelible impression.

Forget the nostalgia. Forget the patriotism. Forget the "old soldier" sentimentality. Forget the "greatest generation" hype. It is simply that the most significant event in one's life and in the recent history of our nation deserves to be told.

It is intended as a gift from my generation for the benefit of one's children, grandchildren, army buddies, colleagues, maybe even the casual reader, and the Eisenhower Center Collection of WWII memoirs in New Orleans.

While no wars are truly good, this war was "good" in the sense that we understood the monstrous evil of Nazi Germany, Fascist Italy and Imperial Japan and what it would portend if they prevailed. As a nation we were united in our commitment to unconditional surrender and victory. Everyone I knew contributed to the war effort in some fashion by serving in the military, working in war factories, buying war bonds, accepting rationing of gas, tires, food and shoes, knitting socks, making bandages, foregoing many luxuries, or faithfully writing letters to loved ones at an army post or overseas.

In the light of our later experience in Vietnam it is hard to conceive of the total willingness of young men to join the war effort voluntarily and enthusiastically. In my high school fraternity of 25 fellows all but one served without hesitation in the military, and incredibly all survived the war, though several were wounded and one was a POW. The one individual who did not serve was disqualified by a medical problem, but wanted to enlist and argued repeatedly and unsuccessfully with the recruiting offices of every one of the services to take him. He felt shamed and unworthy because he could not serve.

I did what my country asked of me willingly. I went where they sent me with no questions. I did my duty with the conviction that it was critical to the future of our nation and my loved ones. There was never a doubt that Eisenhower's "Crusade in Europe" was justified and morally right. Over a half century later I am still proud to have served in the U.S. Army's European Theater of Operations and to have done my part to reach V-E day. I have never had a question that I owed these years and my service to my country. Any other conclusion is unthinkable.

I need to express my gratitude to various individuals whose contributions have enhanced this book. Duane Albro and Louis G. Good preserved the records of the 105th Port Marine Maintenance Co. and Louis created a definitive company history. Roy McKernan and Roy Stephens clarified the significance and details of our work in Antwerp. Ray Buehler provided several key photos. Robert Bell, the youngest guy in the 105th, personifies its spirit and organized company reunions that energized my writing. George "Umpie" Umstead and Morgan "Bud" Ketchum were good buddies and reviewed my recollections of those early days at Camp Wheeler. The anonymous members of the British Civil Defence unit in Antwerp kept, published and provided the author with the record of the terrible V-bomb assault. Bart Verreth of the Statistics Department, Antwerp Port Authority, searched the Port archives and uncovered the wartime ship traffic data. Allan Millett, the author of the best book on World War II, *A War to be Won*, provided motivation and inspiration through his writing.

Clint Greenleaf was totally helpful in making this book a reality.

Fortuitously, my late parents, Alice and Launcelot Havens, my sister, Jane H. Johnson, and my wife, Virginia, preserved all of my wartime correspondence to them, well over 300 letters, which have amplified and verified my memories of those years. Virginia persuaded me to write the book and offered continual encouragement and on-target critiques.

One final thought: creating this memoir has been a totally rewarding effort filled with fun, fulfillment, learning and great memories of those long-past days when we were so young. Even better, in re-reading all of our letters, I fell in love with Virginia all over again.

George N. Havens, Bozeman, Montana

• • •

Japan attacked Pearl Harbor on 7 December 1941, called "a date that will live in infamy" by President Franklin D. Roosevelt.

We Made the Headlines Possible

*The Critical Contribution of
the Rear Echelon in World War II*

INTRODUCTION

· · · · · · · ·
·

This commentary focuses on an under-reported aspect of World War II, the contribution of those GIs who served not on the front lines but in the rear areas. They did not make the headlines; they made the headlines possible.

Clearly, the combat soldiers who endured incredible hardships, displayed immense courage, and won the battles deserve the headlines. But behind their brave exploits were the steadfast efforts of the rear echelon soldiers. Their contributions have been under-reported given the preponderance of personnel involved, their relative contribution to the total war effort, and the image that exists that their work was marginal at best and without danger.

Author Doris Kearns Goodwin utilized a parallel approach in writing *No Ordinary Time. Franklin & Eleanor Roosevelt: The Home Front in World War II.*[1] There were many books on the war itself, its leaders, its strategies and its battles, but she chose to fill a void by creating a comprehensive chronicle of the home front during that epochal period.

The reality of the American Army in World War II was that it required at least two service force individuals to support one soldier in a frontline combat unit. These rear-area GIs performed the essential logistical functions of acquisition, warehousing and transportation of food, munitions, equipment, and supplies as well as communications, construction, medical care, military police, intelligence, and other necessary jobs. They ensured that each division in active operations received the 600 to 700 tons of supplies they needed *each day*.[2] Ultimately at war's end there would be 91 divisions in Europe under General Eisenhower: 61 infantry, 25 armored and five airborne.

Many books have been written about the Allies grand strategy, the dramatic battles of Stalingrad, Normandy and The Bulge, the exploits of various combat units, the bold audacity of Patton, and the heavy casualties suffered by frontline units. Less attention has been paid to the great majority of army personnel who were "rear echelon," whose individual and collective efforts supported and made possible the victories of the combat troops.

Lt. General William C. Pagonis led the 40,000 men and women who ran theater logistics for the Persian Gulf War. He created a memorable expression of the critical mission and contribution of the support function: "Good logistics is combat power."[3]

The pre-eminent German general, Erwin Rommel, the "Desert Fox," would have agreed with that assessment. "The bravest men can do nothing without guns, the guns nothing without ammunition," he once said. "The battle is fought and decided by the quartermasters before the shooting begins."[4]

Throughout the many historical books on World War II there are multiple examples of decisions made, actions taken or delayed, battles won or lost, and strategies revised based on logistics. In this book you will find the consequences of the protracted delay in opening the key Port of Antwerp, now called "the blunder at Antwerp," and the resultant impact on the supply situation in the European Theater of Operations. The ultimate logistical contribution of Antwerp is now seen as of prime importance to the final Allied victory in Europe.

I was not a hero. I did not go into Omaha Beach on D-Day. I never fired at the enemy. But most guys in the army never did these things either, even in frontline units. The findings of the combat historian S.L.A. "Slam" Marshall revealed that only 15 to 30% of WW II infantry riflemen fired their weapons in battle. [5]

For every frontline infantryman there were multiple rear-area soldiers in various roles supporting his combat efficiency. I was one of those, making sure that supplies, ammunition, guns and equipment were unloaded from ships and moved to combat divisions.

What makes my rear-echelon story different is the fact that our company was under sustained attack by enemy airplanes and a barrage of V-bombs with no opportunity to shoot back. The six-month German aerial and V-bomb assault on Antwerp killed 4,483 and wounded 7,192 — a total of 11,675 casualties, equivalent to over 75% of an American infantry division. [6]

This commentary relates two intertwined stories. The first is the saga of the Port of Antwerp, its capture, its long-delayed opening, its contribution to shortening the war in Europe, and its bombardment by German V-weapons. This singular episode of the war is infused with the second story, a highly personal insight into the reality, frustration, uncertainty, humor and danger of the rear-area military experience.

This then is my recollection of how we made the headlines possible. It is a micro rather than a macro report — presenting the unforgettable experience of one individual in one support company in one location. It relates the training, travels, assignments and actions of a rear-echelon soldier culminating in the epochal struggle to capture, open and operate the Port of Antwerp despite the desperate and determined efforts of the Germans to halt its usage.

• • • •

• • • •

The Germans used two types of V-weapons, the V-1 cruise missile or flying bomb, often called the "buzz bomb," and the V-2 rocket bomb, a true ballistic missile. These introduced a new type of warfare against which there was no effective defense. They were primitive devices, not very accurate, but their one-ton warheads were devastating against cities and civilian populations.

• • • •

CHAPTER ONE

How It All Started

It has been over a half century, but my experiences in World War II are still clear, vivid, and quite detailed.

While I have always had a good memory, the impact of those experiences must have created deep, indelible tracks in the long-term memory of my brain. While they were unique and profound, it was undoubtedly the unexpected aspect of them that made then so unforgettable. After all, one expects to grow up, graduate from high school, enter college, have a special girl friend, get married and have kids, and do all the other normal, natural things of life in America.

But one does not expect to get plucked from this comfortable existence and be suddenly and totally immersed in the rigid regimentation of military life. For a recent civilian it is a bizarre life with its discipline and close order drill, its traditions and uniforms, its sharp class distinctions between officers and enlisted men, its boring regularity and repetition, its lack of privacy and personal concern, its insistence on military "courtesy" (saluting) and unthinking obedience, its unpredictability on when, where, how and with whom you will serve, its all-male environment and arbitrary orders, and its ever-present exposure to danger and death.

My experiences changed me in many ways. I grew physically stronger, mentally tougher and more resilient. I became a more self-confident, self-reliant individual who could cope with the uncertainties, the mindlessness, the "chicken shit" orders, the boredom, the physical discomfort, and the homesickness of army life. I was exposed to a broad array of men who did not always share my values and viewpoints. I absorbed the basics of good leadership by seeing examples of both first-rate and abysmal leadership. And I assuredly was forced to defer gratification of my hopes and wishes.

From age 18 to 21 it was a dramatically different life that I experienced. I learned to be a good soldier. I kept my "nose clean." I mastered the intricacies of the Manual of Arms. I became skilled at shooting, saluting, standing in line, shining boots, swallowing K and C rations, shoving a bayonet into straw dummies, standing at attention, sleeping under noisy conditions, and surviving.

In the intervening years since the war, I completed my engineering and management education with honors, pursued an exciting, rewarding career in advertising, married my high school sweetheart and had an enviable family life with three sons, traveled extensively, and created a splendid "Shangri-La" second home in Montana. But those three years in World War II had the greatest impact on my life.

• • •

CHAPTER TWO

• • • • •
• • •

A Young College Kid Enlists in the Army

The direct involvement of the United States in World War II began with the Japanese attack on Pearl Harbor on 7 December 1941 and Hitler's declaration of war on the U.S. on 11 December 1941.

My involvement in this war started almost exactly one year later on 1 December 1942 as I signed up for the Enlisted Reserve Corps (ERC) of the U.S. Army.

At that time I was an 18-year-old, first-semester freshman studying engineering at Case School of Applied Science (later to become Case Institute of Technology and now the Case School of Engineering, Case Western Reserve University) in Cleveland, Ohio. I had graduated from Shaw High School, East Cleveland, Ohio in June 1942 and then spent the summer working in a Thompson Products (now TRW) war plant inspecting aircraft fuel pumps on the swing shift, 3 pm to 11 pm, seven days a week before matriculating at Case. I was dating my high school sweetheart, Virginia Ann Councell. Our family resided in East Cleveland during its then halcyon days and included my parents, Launcelot and Alice, and my older sister, Jane, whose husband James B. Johnson served as a naval officer in the Pacific Theater.

In early fall we assembled in the large lecture hall in the Rockefeller Physics Building on the Case campus to hear presentations by representatives from the Army, Navy, Air Corps and Marines. They first reminded us that we were exposed to the ongoing draft of young men to serve in the military and that civilians in college would not merit deferment. Yet they wanted us to stay in college to provide the future officers and technically trained men that the war effort would need. A prolonged war was anticipated before victory could be achieved, after all at that point the Allies had won no major, decisive victories. Anglo-American forces in North Africa were stalemated, Stalingrad was still undecided, Japanese offensive thrusts in the Pacific had been blunted by the victories at Coral Sea and Midway but the island-hopping campaign was yet to come, and the Overlord landings in Normandy had no definite timetable.

The solution they advised was for us to join one of the reserve corps of the four branches where we could then remain in college but be insulated from the draft. Since my myopic eyesight would not enable me to pass the physicals for the Navy, Air Corps or Marines, I chose the Army. I passed the army physical (I was warm!), signed the necessary papers, and acquired my Army Service Number 15358862, the initial "1" designating an *enlistee* while draftees were given numbers starting with "3" …an important differentiation in one's status since *voluntarily enlisting* was clearly superior to being *forcibly drafted*. This was especially evident each month on pay day when everyone lined up in front of the pay table with rank and senority given priority — and *enlistees* lined up ahead of *draftees*. This gave those of us with serial numbers starting with "1" a fine opportunity to hassle the draftees.

Thinking that I had resolved my military service problems, I blithely pursued my studies in calculus, physics, chemistry, engineering drawing, argument and debate, analytical geometry, and physical education. Surviving the first semester, I moved into the spring semester with more confidence,

The girl I left behind: Virginia "Ginnie" Councell. Photo was used by an Antwerp artist to create a memorable portrait painting of her.

was initiated into Phi Delta Theta, and continued dating Virginia who wore my fraternity pin. What could be better? The war news improved with the victory at Stalingrad, successes in North Africa and hopes for better news from the Pacific.

. . . .

WE MADE THE HEADLINES POSSIBLE

• • • • • •

CHAPTER THREE

The Call to Active Duty

But the unpredictable Army had a surprise for me and many others: Special Orders No. 110 from HQ, Fifth Service Command, Fort Hayes, Columbus, Ohio — my call to active duty and an order to report on 22 May 1943 for transport to Camp Perry, Ohio. Case cooperated and enabled me to finish the freshman year before leaving.

While my folks treated Ginnie and me to a farewell steak dinner at the Hickory Grill, a fine restaurant on Short Vincent in Cleveland, I quickly began to learn that my life was going to be radically different. Before departing I had a front tooth extracted which left a hole in my gum and a gap in my smile. On her way to Ann Arbor to matriculate at Michigan, Ginnie returned my Phi Delt pin. I left behind all my civilian clothes, my home, my room, my beloved jazz records, my books, everything that was familiar to me. I said goodbye to my friends and fraternity brothers, relatives and neighbors, and at age 18 went down to the Armed Forces Induction Station in the Terminal Tower.

A train took us to Camp Perry over near Toledo, which was a first stop for new GIs. My impressions of Perry are of a confusing start to my army career. They issued uniforms, equipment, barracks bags and dog tags, inspected us, injected us, read us the Articles of War, tested us for blood and brains, gave us menial jobs to do, sold us $10,000 GI insurance policies, gave us typhoid shots, showed us a movie on sex hygiene, had us shoveling coal, told us in that famous army phrase "you'll be sorry," and otherwise confused and harassed us for a week. I wasn't sure we could ever win the war this way.

An especially challenging activity at Perry was learning how to put my ID on everything I'd been issued. One's army ID consists of the initial of your last name and the last four numbers of your service number. Hence, my ID was "H-8862" which I lettered or stenciled on everything I owned: duffel bag, barracks bag, foot locker, clothes, canteen cover, all my gear. It was a warning to everyone: H-8862 meant it belonged to Havens. It was my claim to all my earthly army possessions including my underwear.

The most memorable event at Perry was finding that George Joseph "Umpie" Umstead was also there. George and I had gone through school together (grades 5 through 12), been acolytes together at St. Paul's Episcopal Church, East Cleveland, been in the same high school fraternity, and had much in common, like a love of singing, good jokes and girls. I even called him "Brother." After the war he would be an usher in our wedding party. We had also been a formidable debate team at Shaw High School, although we were once criticized by a judge as "the most bombastic, sarcastic, uninformed, misinformed, diabolical and scheming debate team he had ever judged." My recollection is that we won the debate. It was appropriate preparation for George's career as a lawyer and mine as an advertising executive.

Finding Umpie among the nameless GI faces was a godsend. Even better, we then discovered Morgan Zeising "Bud" Ketchum and formed a triumvirate. Bud was a Shaker High graduate whose father and uncle were prominent in East Cleveland business and whose aunt and uncle were pillars of St. Paul's Church. Incredibly Bud and I would later meet up numerous times in the States and overseas. Now I had two buddies to make the army experience easier and less formidable.

Soon they loaded us onto a troop train that headed south, we were going to Camp Wheeler, an infantry replacement training center (IRTC), near Macon, Georgia. We picked up additional cars to our train as we moved through Ohio, Kentucky, Tennessee and Georgia until we had some 1000 soldiers, all of whom it turned out were college students. The plan, which we would only learn later, was to put us through basic training, then send us back to college under the Army Specialized Training Program (ASTP).

The ride in day coaches was long, hot, boring, uncomfortable, tiring. As I recall, all we did was talk, play cards, read, sing, doze, and wonder where the hell we were going and what it would be like. Our coach car was adequate as were the L&N cars we added, but the Central of Georgia cars seemed like ones that had survived Sherman's march to the sea.

· · · · ·

Long-term friend, George J. Umstead, who shared infantry basic training but ended the war in a German prison camp.

George Umstead
Secretary

CHAPTER FOUR

The Summer of '43 in Georgia

On 3 June 1943 the train pulled right into Camp Wheeler on a siding and we disembarked, happy to be off the train, but dazed by the hot Georgia sun and wondering what came next. Then came the shouted order, "Line up and count off by fours." I believe it was Umpie who said to Bud and me, let's line up so that we are every fourth person. At that count-off we three were each "Ones" who were told to report to Company A area. At Company A area the first sergeant repeated the lineup and count-off procedure, this time we were "Twos" and told to report to the Second Platoon building. At the Second Platoon, Sgt. McClendon reiterated the exercise, this time we were "Fours" and assigned to the Fourth Squad. So Umstead, Ketchum and Havens went through 13 weeks of basic training together in the Fourth Squad, Second Platoon, Company A of the 7th Training Battalion. It sure helped!

The structure of an infantry training battalion at Camp Wheeler consisted of four companies, each with four platoons, and each 50-man platoon had four squads of 12 men each. So the Havens-Ketchum-Umstead trio represented 3 out of the 12 guys in our squad, incredible odds when you think about it.

Shortly thereafter we lined up in the shade of our two-story platoon barracks to meet our platoon lieutenant. His arrival and his impact were totally memorable. His first words to us were: "My name is Wilson. I'm 19 years old. I'm a **first lieutenant**. I come from Harlan County, Kentucky. I run this platoon. If anyone disagrees with that, step out cause we're going to settle it right now." No one budged. I guess we all knew about the reputation of "Bloody Harlan" County with its fights, feuds, murders and give-no-quarter Appalachian lifestyle.

Lt. Wilson was an extraordinary individual and a superb leader of men. He was tough and demanding but fair. He insisted that we be the best platoon not only in Company A but of all the 16 platoons in the battalion! He led us through those 13 weeks in a way that earned our admiration and respect. He led by example doing all the difficult things first. In fact, he loved the hazardous exercises such as the Infiltration Course, Combat Course, Village Fighting and others, and volunteered to lead the other Company A platoons through these tough training requirements.

One metric of platoon excellence was the daily barracks inspection which occurred while we were off doing calisthenics, close order drill, bayonet practice or other infantry fundamentals. The winning platoon was marked by a red flag bestowed by the Company Commander, Captain Swisher, after his inspection. Out of four platoons we won more than 50% of the time. If the red flag was not on our barracks as we marched back to the company area for lunch, Wilson ordered us to correct any shortcomings, then went to the HQ to harangue Swisher, often bringing him back to our barracks to see how superior ours was. I think Leo Durocher and Billy Martin learned umpire baiting tactics from Wilson.

Lt. Wilson held an optional dirty fighting class in the gym at 10 am on Sundays; he clearly wanted us to be prepared for the worst. At this time our training cadre included a Corporal Campbell who was a bully and a rotten guy, pulling his rank on everyone and making our life miserable. For a particular Sunday class, Wilson asked Campbell to be present and used him as a human punching bag to demonstrate all his "dirty" kicks, takedowns, holds, and maneuvers. He worked Campbell over somewhat brutally to the delight of the class. The next day Campbell applied for a transfer to another unit and was gone. It was a powerful example of how Lt. Wilson resolved problems and stood up for his men, characteristics that any of us would want in a combat leader.

The 13-week basic training cycle covers all of the fundamental skills, knowledge and conditioning that an infantry fighting man needs. Infantry training was extensive given that foot soldiers required the least technical training of the various branches of the army. Each day was divided into a morning and an afternoon segment with a precise schedule for each activity. Lunch might be at the company mess or in the field.

The instruction included calisthenics, close order drill, manual of arms, rifle practice, bayonet drill, map reading, estimating distances, using a compass, field sanitation procedures with the Lister bag, latrine, and slit trench, use of entrenching tools, maintenance of equipment, poison gas drills, night operations, camouflage and concealment, recognition of American, Allied and enemy aircraft and armored vehicles, outpost duty, military courtesy and discipline, first aid, and others.

Weapons training was a major focus. Each of us had our own M-1 Garand rifle which went everywhere with us. We learned the basic firing positions: prone, kneeling, sitting, squatting, and standing. We learned to load, fire, reload, unload, and clean our weapon as well as disassemble and reassemble it in total darkness. We zeroed our M-1s, a procedure where one adjusts and aligns the rifle sights, both elevation and windage, with the bullet trajectory to ensure that you hit what you are aiming at.

This requires a sequence of shots with each shot marked on the target by the guys in the rifle pits and then an adjustment to the sights to correct for the inaccuracy until the shots all hit dead in the bull's-eye. We had extended target practice on the range so that one's shoulder got bruised and tender from the rifle kickback even though this was less severe from the M-1 Garand than the '03 Springfield rifle.

In one exercise, a rapid fire drill where you had to start standing, assume a prone position, fire the bullet in the chamber, reload an ammo clip, and fire the remaining eight bullets all in 51 seconds at a one-foot bull's-eye 300 yards away — I scored a "perfect" with all shots in the bull's-eye. This earned me a Sharpshooter rating.

The training and this accomplishment served me well. While I never had the chance to fire a weapon at the enemy (as you will learn, they did all the firing at us), I had an opportunity to put my skill to work at age 75. On a Museum of the Rockies canoe trip retracing the route of Lewis & Clark along the Missouri River Breaks in Montana, the tour leader, Jack Taylor, demonstrated the loading and firing of a black powder rifle. He then set up a soda can about 50 yards away and challenged the group to hit it. Others fired from a standing position and all missed. I immediately assumed a kneeling position and blew the can away. In a way, I guess the Germans were fortunate I never aimed at them.

We were taught and fired the twelve basic infantry weapons: M-1 Garand, M-1 carbine, '03 Springfield rifle, rifle grenade launcher, hand grenade, .45 cal. pistol, .30 cal. machine gun, .50 cal. machine gun, 60-mm mortar, 81-mm mortar, Browning Automatic Rifle (BAR) and the bazooka.

The fact that we were "college kids" upset some of the training schedules and dismayed the blue-collar cadre. In one instance where a time allocation had been established for a class to teach us how to disassemble and reassemble our M-1 Garand rifles in the dark, we mastered this in half the time, leaving the cadre wondering how to use the remaining time.

We were put through various combat courses: Infiltration, crawling under barbed wire with live bullets overhead; Village Fighting, to learn how to move through an enemy-held area; Quick Reaction: where one had to fire at unsuspected targets that popped up; Squad Firefight, where the full squad fires at targets some 400-600 yards away in a combat setting; Squad Maneuvers, learning how to advance under fire; and others.

Of course we learned to march. Since we were "college kids" the blue-collar permanent cadre gave us an extra tough time. Unlike other training battalions, we marched with all equipment: rifle, steel helmet and liner, full field pack, gas mask, canteen and first aid kit on the required sequence of 6-8 marches which started out at 2-1/2 miles and ended up at 25 miles. We marched four abreast in squad columns, the tallest in front, grading down to the shortest in the rear. Our pace was standard army route march: 106 paces a minute or three miles per hour. We would go 2-1/2 miles, then have a ten-minute break.

The cadre were humane in one sense. With the extreme heat and humidity in Georgia in the summer, they arranged for some marches to be done at night. These night marches had some rare experiences. We would depart about 8 pm and head out of camp along the assigned route. In so doing we would pass right by the POW compound filled with German and Italian prisoners from Rommel's Afrika Corps. It was more efficient to bring them to the States in ships that would otherwise return empty than it was to ship all of the food, clothing, medicine and their other needs to Europe or Africa. At any rate as we trudged by loaded down with our gear and facing a long tiring night, we saw them relaxing, singing, smoking, playing soccer, having a fine time which always prompted the question, "Who the hell is winning this war?"

On the longer night marches some of our platoon members, especially those who marched in the inner two columns, learned to fall asleep while walking, depending on their buddies to keep then headed straight. In preparation for these marches the mess hall arranged for coffee as a caffeine injection to keep us awake. I'd never had coffee but with lots of encouragement I had a canteen cup of coffee laced with cream and sugar. One would never confuse the army version of coffee with Starbucks best but it did its job — I was totally zipped that night, bright-eyed and bushy-tailed for that march and slept little upon our return to camp. Thus, drinking coffee was another learning experience from the army.

• • •

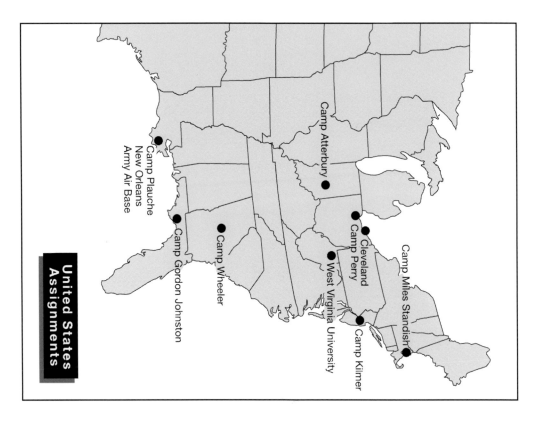

United States Assignments

- Camp Plauche
  New Orleans
  Army Air Base
- Camp Gordon Johnston
- Camp Wheeler
- Camp Atterbury
- Cleveland
  Camp Perry
- West Virginia University
- Camp Kilmer
- Camp Miles Standish

United States Assignments: 15 months of infantry basic, specialized and advanced training preceded departure for Europe from the Boston Port of Embarkation.

CHAPTER FIVE

• • • • • • •

The Army is the Army, You'll Be Sorry!

My memory is that the training was rigorous, especially in the unrelenting heat and humidity of the summer of '43. Often our days started at 4:30 a.m. and ended at dark. Some guys suffered heat stroke and heat exhaustion, everyone had heat rashes, jock itch, chigger bites, mosquito bites, sun burn, aching muscles, sweat-soaked clothes and homesickness. A bright moment each day was mail call when one of the non-commissioned officers (non-coms) would distribute the mail to an anxious group of GIs, calling out each name and getting an eager response of "Here" or "Yo." Some non-coms would add some humor by smelling an envelope with feminine writing and adding a comment like "Hey, this one must be a real sweetie."

The food was bland with many heavy meat-potatoes-gravy meals, lots of pork, but most of us were too hot and exhausted to care. We just needed fuel for energy. We sat at picnic-type tables of eight or ten, ate family style from heaping bowls of food, and griped about the training regimen, the weather, and life in general. To bring order out of chaos during our meals we sternly enforced table discipline and jumped on those who broke the rules. Whoever took the last helping from a bowl, thereby "cinching it" had to get up, go to the kitchen and get more. If someone took a piece of bread and did not take hold of the serving plate, it would be dropped directly onto his meal, splat, to the accompaniment of great laughter. Short-stopping of a requested serving dish by taking your helping as it was being passed along to the requester was forbidden.

Meals in the field were usually C rations or K rations, not much of an accomplishment for a country that invented the atom bomb. K rations contained a D ration chocolate bar originally designed so that it would not melt in the African desert operations. The only problem was that it would not melt in your mouth either. Each K ration and C ration contained a mini pack of cigarettes, so some American firms were already working to build their post-war markets.

One of the famous events was the exercise at the infamous Area K. After marching out to the area, we ran squad maneuvers all day on limited water ration, one canteen for the entire day of oppressive heat. This involved hiding on the ground, jumping up and running 20-30 feet as fast as possible, falling down amidst the chiggers, then repeating this down one side of a hill and up the other side...all day. Then we marched five miles to our bivouac area, the last stretch being a bushwhack up the side of a hill that seemed endless. Halfway up my legs and water-deprived body quit, but Umstead was behind me and he put his hand on my butt and pushed me to the top. His muscular legs had been well-developed as a guard on the Shaw High football team. I collapsed in my tent and might still be there but Umpie and Bud did some reconnoitering in a nearby farmer's field and came back with a juicy watermelon. I owe them my life!

Barracks life was both humorous and weird. We were clearly outnumbered by the resident battalion of cockroaches. And getting a good night's rest in a room with 24 other guys takes training to tune out the disturbances. One such sleep-depriver was an unpopular Russian fellow, Macaroff, who kept powdering himself and slathering on body lotions with interminable slapping of his body every night after lights out. Despite vigorous criticism he refused to stop this noisy ritual which must have had a religious or ethnic imperative for there were no girls to impress.

Luckily we had the irrepressible Mel Goldsmith from Brooklyn who kept us sane with his perverted sense of humor. He would regale us in the early morning as we struggled into our fatigues about the troops of cockroaches he had observed marching up and down the floor during the night in perfect drill order. He would hold court in the barracks to distribute the clothing that was returned from the laundry, totally breaking us up as he displayed woolen socks that had shrunk to a miniature, unwearable size. Whenever our morale hit bottom his spontaneous wit was a marvelous tonic to keep us going. As the training weeks in 1943 went by and it dawned on us that we were going to be in the army for "a long, long time" with no end in sight, he would lift our spirits by having us sing "I'll be home for Christmas in *1993!*" One of his favorites was leading us in the singing of "I'm Dreaming of a White *Mistress*" (instead of Christmas). He was always doing something zany, thank goodness.

The worst event of the summer was contracting infectious diarrhea and being confined to the post hospital. When you go into the hospital in the army you have to pack up all of your gear and turn it in at the supply room. You do this no matter how sick or weak you are which is supposed to discourage malingerers. They put me on a diet of bismuth and paregoric but nothing helped and I knew that if I missed more than a week of training, I would have to take basic all over again. I lay there dehydrated, debilitated and disgusted, not able to eat, and not getting better. After a week I talked my way out of the hospital, went back to our barracks, took a big dose of Sal Hepatica which almost turned me inside out, but halted the infection. Weak and woozy from the experience I rejoined my comrades, not realizing that this incident would alter my army career.

The experience of living on an army post was a new one for me. While Wheeler was a wartime camp and not a permanent facility like Fort Benning, it still followed all of the military traditions, regulations and discipline of the regular U.S. Army. Each part of the day was announced by bugle calls over the P.A. system: Reveille, Mess, Retreat, Tattoo, Taps and others. I found all these calls which the army has long used to be memorable and lyrical, but Tattoo, a haunting call which summons troops to their quarters at night, was a favorite. These traditional bugle calls add certainty, predictability and finality to each day.

Camp Wheeler was named for the Confederate General Joseph B. Wheeler, a cavalry commander who had the nasty job of trying to contain and confront Gen. William Tecumseh Sherman and his Union army on the march from Atlanta to the sea. The army displayed unusual diplomacy in its bow to Southern loyalties as it named many of its facilities in the South for Confederate heros: Fort Bragg, Fort Lee, Camp Gordon, Camp Jackson, Fort Hood, and others, as well as Wheeler.

Camp Wheeler was one of the 46 army camps that were completed in the spring of 1941 by the Quartermaster Corps as the country mobilized for the anticipated war. I marveled at how quickly the total camp infrastructure of barracks, headquarters, chapels, mess hall, Bachelor Officer Quarters, gym, rifle range, combat training courses, PX, et al had been erected here in the boonies of Georgia. Given the rural location, we marched, it seemed, over all of the back roads of that part of Georgia, past mile after mile of peach and pecan orchards. It seems probable that some of these roads were the same ones that Sherman's army had traversed. These roads were red Georgia clay which our marching feet churned up into clouds of fine red dust, so thick that often we had to wear handkerchiefs over our mouths and noses. The combination of red clay dust and GI sweat produced some strange faces.

One of the best events at Wheeler was meeting Alexander Constantine Georgalakis from Portland, Oregon who was in another squad of the 2nd Platoon. Georg, as I called him, embodied strong Greek traits: darkly handsome, intelligent, athletic, arrogant with a short fuse, and a smooth operator with the ladies. He and I would become close comrades in the year ahead and his friendship added much to my army experience.

Despite the people all around you there is a built-in loneliness in army life, so having a good friend like Georg to share difficulties and doubts, hopes and dreams made a huge difference.

Evenings were usually spent quietly trying to cool off and recoup for the next day, perhaps sitting on the small porch off our second floor with a pint of vanilla ice cream and a coke from the PX, good tasting and lots of sugar for energy. Or writing letters home to Ginnie, Mom and Dad, sister Jane, or some of the high school fraternity fellows whose addresses we'd obtained. Or reminiscing about home, high school, girls, good times — the fact that Umpie knew Ginnie well was an immense help. Or strolling around the other company areas to see guys we knew like the Friedman brothers, Morrie and Skip (later a German POW), and reminiscing about our pre-army lives in Cleveland and our plans for after the war.

. . . .

CHAPTER SIX

Basic Training is Over, So Back to College

• • • • • • •

Finally, after all the marching, close order drill, classes and calisthenics, the 13-week basic was over. We were gratified to receive a unit commendation from the commanding general of Camp Wheeler which was reported as follows:

Completing their cycle without having a single AWOL case, the 7th training battalion, composed of prospective ASTP candidates rolled up several records which are unique…On the 20-mile march, not a single soldier fell out…On the range more than 96% of the trainees qualified with the majority gaining high scores. General Brown officially commended the battalion on their splendid record of performance.

I had survived June, July and August in Georgia. What next, I wondered. In the army nothing happens until "orders are cut" but we had lots of rumors. An army without rumors or scuttlebutt would be a sorry group. Soon the orders were cut, Umstead and Ketchum along with most of our battalion were going to the University of Alabama at Tuscaloosa for ASTP; because of my hospital stay I was assigned as part of a smaller group to West Virginia University in Morgantown, also for ASTP. So after our initial army experiences together, our close-knit threesome was going to be dissolved, a move which I deeply regretted. I would see Ketchum in New Orleans and overseas but not reunite with Umpie until after the war in 1946.

Our "hospital list" group that went to West Virginia almost ended up with an infantry division involved in advanced training maneuvers in Tennessee before immediately heading overseas. An incompetent personnel clerk had lumped our "hospital" group in with the ASTP "rejects"; it took some desperate intervention by one of our guys who knew a colonel at HQ to get our orders changed. Ultimately our situation went as high as the 4th Service Command HQ in Atlanta to get straightened out. Until our orders were changed Umstead was so mad about my raw deal that he was ready to hit the first officer he encountered.

The Army Specialized Training Program absorbed 140,000 young men at its height.[7] They were sent to more than 200 colleges and universities to study engineering, foreign languages, medicine and dentistry. Selected for their high IQs and previous educational experience, they believed they would eventually be assigned to technical duties requiring such training. Many expected to become officers.[8]

Being a soldier and going to college is a strange phenomenon. My classes at West Virginia were mainly repeats of basic engineering courses I'd already taken at Case. We lived in student dorms and stood a Saturday morning room inspection when quarter coins had to bounce off super-tight blankets and dust had to be non-existent. On one inspection my roommates, Al Hastings, Bob Hawkes (in the Army's alphabetical fixation Havens was sandwiched between them) and I determined to give our C.O. Lt. Dickinson no opportunity to find any faults. Dickinson had been a collegiate heavyweight boxing champion and as he entered our room he immediately sensed the challenge. Windows sparkled, beds were perfect, dust was nowhere, floor was waxed, everything was in its assigned place — we watched with a growing feeling of triumph. Then he pulled out a small pocket knife, went to the corner of the room, bent over to pry some dirt from the corner of the floor, and eyed us with disdain. He'd won, but we concluded that he'd been hit in the head too many times in the boxing ring.

Morgantown was a pleasant small college town laid out, like most of West Virginia, on the side of a hill. It had a USO where we could relax on weekends and dance with the local girls. The best dancer and a real woman's man was my close buddy, Alex "Georg" Georgalakis. Our typical Saturday night routine was to head for the USO for some fun and games with the opposite sex. In short order Georg would have zeroed in on an attractive girl and charmed her with his smooth talk and fancy footwork. He had a good line and worked fast; I envied his technique.

Late on Saturday night after the USO we would hit the nearby hamburg joint for two hamburgers with raw onions and chocolate milk. Unbelievably we survived this weird diet for all our time at WVU.

I was to be in Morgantown for the Fall '43 and Spring '44 quarters at WVU and my parents arranged two delightful interludes. First they drove to Morgantown bringing Ginnie with them and stayed at the Morgan Hotel for a weekend. As I recall we had a picnic in a park north of the town and it was wonderful to see them. On a later occasion I took a bus to Pittsburgh and met them for another brief period. My thoughtful and cooperative father made the hotel reservations, a double for Mom and him, and two *adjoining* single rooms for Ginnie and me. Now that's the kind of Dad to have — he thought that nothing was too good for a serviceman! Well, it turned out to be *nothing*. My Mother would have none of this liaison and was adamant that her future daughter-in-law's reputation not be sullied, so she and Ginnie occupied the single rooms, while I bunked in with Dad. Another fond dream smashed.

I did get a pass to go home over Christmas but getting there wasn't easy. To save money I tried to hitchhike to Pittsburgh where I could get a train for Cleveland. The only car to pick me up was going to Greensburg, 30-40 miles east of Pittsburgh but still on the train route. I finally arrived home, late, cold and tired, but overjoyed to be there. I am sure it was a great reunion, but the holiday and the return are indistinct in my memory. Back at our WVU dorm I celebrated New Year's eve by having my first real drink (at age 19), a rum and Coca-cola. It was so good I wondered why I had waited so long for this treat. Then incredibly I had a seven-day furlough back home to start the year.

The author shared many good times with Alexander "Georg" Georgalakis, shown here with his wartime bride.

In February Georg asked me to join him in a dinner invitation to a Greek home. Upon arrival we were served small glasses of straight whiskey, which immediately improved my opinion of the Greeks. Then we commenced dinner and not realizing what was coming I ate plenty of the first-course spaghetti and wine, then groaned when platters of chicken and dressing were presented and almost died when the main course of pot roast was delivered to the table. I tried to politely decline this course but our hostess responded that it had been prepared "just for the two of you." So I heroically dug in, consumed my share and then staggered through a dessert of apple pie. We ended up with strong, dark Greek coffee that capped the event. It was several days before I wanted to eat again and I now knew what that old adage of "beware of Greeks bearing gifts" meant.

An interesting guy at WVU was Joseph B. Hendrie, who had studied engineering at Wayne State University. Joe was a high-energy, gung-ho soldier, very military, very focused, very committed. When he heard that ASTP would be dissolved and we were headed back to the troops, he started conditioning himself by taking long hikes in the evening with full field pack and other gear up and down those West Virginia hills. In his postwar career he graduated from Case Institute of Technology in 1950 with honors as a physics major. Ultimately he ended up as a top official at the Nuclear Regulatory Commission where he was the person who took charge of the meltdown incident at the Three Mile Island nuclear facility and took a lot of flak over this serious problem.

• • • • •

CHAPTER SEVEN

ASTP Dies and It's Back to the Troops

ASTP was a noble endeavor but it could not withstand the political pressures nor the reality that our two-front war against both Germany and Japan needed more war-zone man-power. So it was shut down in spring of '44 and orders were cut assigning 120,000 ASTP men to active units, 73,000 to the Army Ground Forces (like Umstead) to be used as infantry replacements for depleted divisions and the rest to the Service Forces (like Ketchum and myself).

The *Morgantown Post* editorialized about us:

We would like to set it down here for the record that the community has enjoyed having them and regrets their departure. They have been conspicuously well behaved. Indeed, we do not recall a single instance when their conduct has created any sort of public incident...they proved themselves surprisingly good students.

Once again the rumor mill churned wildly, the most popular notion was that we were going to the Second Army which was on maneuvers in Tennessee. As usual it was wrong. While we were kept in the dark the *Morgantown Post* of 30 March 1944 provided details under a banner headline: "509 Soldiers Leave W.V.U. for New Posts." The *Post* described the previous day's departure of "381 ASTPers on a 6:35 pm ten-car Pullman train destined to join various Transportation Corps harbor-craft companies in New Orleans."[9] It didn't say much for wartime secrecy but it epitomized the army's Mushroom Policy — keep them in the dark and feed them manure.

I was ordered to a "repple depple" (the GI term for a replacement depot) at Camp Plauche, New Orleans. Through an exchange of letters I learned that Bud Ketchum had been assigned to the 1668 Engineer Utility Detachment, a fire fighting company, but George Umstead drew the short straw and ended up in a heavy weapons company of the 423rd Regiment, 106th Infantry Division. To jump ahead for a moment: this bad-luck division shipped over to the European Theater of Operations (ETO) and with no combat experience was moved into the line to defend 26 miles of front. Incredibly it was to be right in the path of Von Rundstedt's Ardennes Offensive, better known as the Battle of the Bulge. Shortly after taking up their positions, German panzer and infantry divisions launched their attack at 5:30 am on 16 December 1944 and with a six-to-one advantage quickly overwhelmed the 106th capturing most of the 422nd and 423rd regiments including Umpie. As he put it, "we were using mortars against their artillery, the famed 88s...there was no chance." He spent the rest of the war in the Bad Orb Stalag before being liberated by the advancing U.S. troops. Barely subsisting on meager rations and sleeping on cold prison floors during the German winter caused him serious health problems which continued after his release.

My repple-depple experience verified the observation of Karl von Clausewitz, Prussian general and historian that "the only certainty about war is its uncertainty." I suppose the army required replacement depots where unassigned soldiers could be quartered until their orders came along. But they were human warehouses; without friends or the support of your unit, without any certainty about when orders would be cut or where you'd end up, without a regular routine to organize your day, they were deadly on morale. The certain uncertainty of the army meant that from day to day you did not know what tomorrow would bring.

I found the Camp Plauche "repple depple" to be a lonely, depressing place as I sat awaiting assignment, wondering what came next, just another GI with a number. Adding to my malaise was the news I received there that my paternal grandfather for whom I was named, George Henry Havens, had died at age 82 in East Cleveland. A dignified man with the usual Havens sense of humor, a long-term Western Union telegrapher, and a 32nd degree Mason, he had been born in Canada and moved to East Cleveland in 1895. I can still see him sitting in his back bedroom listening to the radio broadcasts of the Cleveland Indians baseball games. A frugal man on a modest salary, he owned his own home and the double house next door where I was born.

· · · · ·

CHAPTER EIGHT

The 105th: A Maverick Unit, an Unusual Mission

After days of boredom, orders were cut assigning me to the 105th Port Marine Maintenance Co., part of the Transportation Corps, Army Service Forces, which was organized on 1 March 1944.[10]

On 16 May 1944 the new company was relocated to the New Orleans Army Air Base where the company commenced its initial training, essentially a repeat of my previous basic training, but not as rigorous, tough or disciplined. The 105th was one of some 10 similar companies organized at that time whose mission would be to open, operate and maintain a major port for the receipt of supplies, equipment, materiel, and ammunition. Our unit was basically 200 men and six officers which operated pretty much on its own, although technically assigned to the 13th Major Port Group.

Things got better. In the 105th were a large number of recent draftees out of mills, factories and shipyards with the requisite technical skills such as machinist, rigger, pipefitter, steamfitter, welder, electrician, diver, driver — the things needed for our mission. But there was also a small group of ex-ASTP college guys who formed a supportive clique, including Paul Grady, Duane "Doc" Albro, Ray Buehler, Roy McKernan, Louis

Good, and myself. We had been through basic, knew the army routine, and had many common interests. We had some great adventures in New Orleans with dinner at The Court of the Two Sisters and drinks at lots of bars, toured the French Quarter, rode the streetcars, eyed the girls, and always got back to camp before curfew.

Young-looking ASTPers enjoy mint juleps in New Orleans at The Court of the Two Sisters. (L to R) Duane "Doc" Albro, Ray Buehler, the author; Paul Grady, Roy McKernan.

The first bar-hopping evening became a personal disaster for me. As a novice drinker (only the rum and coke at New Year's), I wanted some suggestions. At the first bar the guy next to me ordered a Tom Collins, so did I. At the next bar I was next to someone else who ordered Seagram's and Seven, so did I. At the

next bar, it was another guy and a different drink. I lost count. But I do know we ended up the evening drinking Cream Brandy Alexanders at Pat O'Brien's. All this after a long, hot day of army training in the sun. On the streetcar ride (out to where our company trucks would pick us up) I clutched one of the vertical poles as the car swayed severely from side to side. All that night in my cot my inebriated mind had me clutching that pole as it rocked back and forth while the bunkroom spun around. The next morning's training activities in the hot sun were too painful to describe. What a baptism!

A signal event occurred shortly after our arrival at this base. We were all called out for the reading of an official bulletin from the War Department: Allied forces had this day landed on the beaches in Normandy, France. It was D-Day, 6 June 1944 and the invasion we had waited for so long was on. Designated as Operation Overlord, it was to be the largest amphibious attack ever launched. Now we would confront Hitler on his own ground in Fortress Europe and learn how successful we could be against the vaunted German army. We all said a silent prayer for all those engaged in this momentous and decisive effort.

Invasion of Normandy on D-Day 1944 as Allied troops land on Sword, Juno, Gold, Omaha and Utah beaches.

Upon completing basic training I had become a Private First Class, so my pay escalated from $50 a month to $56. Then 5 June 1944 marked my modest move up the ranks in grade and pay as I was promoted to Corporal, actually Technician, Grade 5 (T-5) with a monthly stipend of $66. See description of Army Enlisted and Officer Ranks (pages 83-84).

Perhaps the only highlight of the training was the opportunity to earn my Red Cross lifesaving badge in Lake Pontchartrain, much cleaner in 1944 than now. Georgalakis was still around in a different company and he lined up some double dates with a couple of local girls. We saw the movie "Gaslight" with Ingrid Bergman and Charles Boyer, ate dinner at the Roosevelt Hotel, walked in the parks and even rode the streetcar named "Desire." Nice girls but nothing like those special ones at dear old Shaw High.

On 1-2 July 1944 we moved to Camp Gordon Johnston located east of Apalachicola near Carrabelle on the Florida-Gulf of Mexico panhandle, a dreadful camp. Don't take my word. In his book, *A General's Life*, General Omar N. Bradley declared:

Camp Gordon Johnston was the most miserable Army installation I had seen since my days in Yuma, Arizona, ages past. It had been hacked out of palmetto scrub along a bleak stretch of beach...The man who selected that site should have been court-martialed for stupidity.[11]

The barracks had sand floors, so we had sand in everything — beds, pillows, footlockers, clothes, hair. The messhall had no seats, just higher-than normal tables and we stood up to eat — we could never figure out the purpose of this awkward arrangement and it sure didn't make the food taste any better. The camp was sited in a scrub pine forest near the beach with Dog Island offshore to permit amphibious assault training, a reality which came as a nasty surprise. We hoped we weren't going to assault anything.

During the training period I was one of ten men selected to take special instruction in chemical warfare protection and anti-aircraft practice with the Browning .50 caliber machine gun and tracer bullets. This was a welcome diversion and a nice honor.

The ongoing full-company training by our uninspiring officers was tedious, ineffective and somewhat lost on our craft and tech trades guys who never did get the hang of close order drill or smart marching. So the captain, normally an intelligent guy, made a dumb, dumb decision. Billeted near us was a black company whose marching and drill skills were classy, showy, and precise. So he invited them to parade up and down in front of us to show us how it should really be done. They turned it on with snappy precision, shouted responses to the orders, slap-ping of rifles, and rhythm, rhythm, rhythm. They put on a good show — but the captain had forgotten that a large contingent of his men in the 105th were Southerners. The Rebels were furi-ous, resentful, insulted. As was predictable, the marching did not improve.

Another inspired move by our wonderful officers was to issue us brand new boots to take overseas, and then immediately schedule a ten-mile march. Upon completing this hike the backs of my lower legs were rubbed raw and bleeding. By the time I got overseas I had bad ulcerations and blood poisoning that took antibiotics to clear up. It was painful, uncomfortable and totally unnecessary.

Perhaps the only bright spot of this two-month stay was the weekend chance to head over to the well-known fancy resort at Wakulla Springs. There we could swim in pure spring water, relax, check out the bathing suits, eat some decent food and re-call what civilian life was like. As with all good things, it didn't last. At the end of the day we had to return to Camp Gordon Johnston and its ubiquitous sand.

Before leaving this camp most of the company received welcome furloughs to get home and see their loved ones. But this opportunity did not end up happily for everyone. One individual returned from his Alabama home after discovering that his wife was "shacking up" with another man. He was so humiliated and depressed that he attempted to hang himself that night in the barracks, but was found and cut down before ending his life. In standard army practice he was then transferred out of the company.

• • •

Good-bye USA. Hello ETO.

Soon more orders were cut and on 20 August 1944 we proceeded to Camp Miles Standish near Boston, a major Port of Embarkation (POE). We were going overseas. There were no tears as we bid the funky Camp Gordon Johnston goodbye. Our troop train headed up the east coast and I can recall us going past Washington, D.C. late in the day and seeing the Washington Monument and the Lincoln and Jefferson Memorials. This added a needed touch of inspiration to our trip.

We moved into our temporary quarters at the camp whose command team was accustomed to more conventional army units and clearly wasn't prepared for a maverick outfit like ours. In a foolish move they put our company on K.P. in the consolidated mess which served some 3000 soldiers. In preparation for lunch we peeled potatoes, mopped the floors, cleaned the tables and got our detailed instructions for manning the food serving line. "Each GI is to get ONE PORK CHOP, JUST ONE" we were sternly told, but our guys heard that as a challenge. As the hungry soldiers moved through the mess line, our guys piled on the chops, as many as anyone wanted…and then hollered "More chops, more chops!" as the situation spun out of control. The cooks feverishly retrieved more pork chops from the coolers, quickly grilled them, and rushed them up to the serving line. It looked like a scene out of a Keystone Kops silent movie. When lunch was over we had given out some 10,000 pork chops — and set a new camp record. Our guys were good!

We went through all the last minute checks of injections, medical records, clothing, equipment, and weapons, We got instructions on shipboard behavior and discipline. We were cautioned not to tell anyone, even parents, where we were and when we would leave — "Loose lips sink ships," you know. And then we were ready to do the army thing — wait.

While waiting Paul Grady, a close friend among the ASTPers, and I got a 36-hour pass and took off. Paul took us first to his home in Wollaston, Boston suburb, where we got our adventure off to a fast start with several Southern Comforts. Even though we had been cautioned not to call home and reveal our location, Paul's gruff, good-natured father insisted that I phone my parents at his expense. Early the next morning we drove down to Point Judith, Rhode Island and sat on the beach with Paul's then-current girlfriend, who was beautiful by definition (Paul had frequently voiced his intention to marry the richest, best-looking girl he could find). Later we had a delicious lobster dinner at the Grady's seashore home on Narragansett Bay. Then we had to head back to Camp Miles Standish, but en route we stopped at the famous Biltmore Hotel in Providence for a farewell drink, and made it to camp just in time. A great final 36 hours in the U.S. enhanced by the ever-present awareness that we did not know when or if we would ever see the U.S. again.

On 29 August 1944 loaded down with all our gear we staggered up a steep gangplank and boarded the *U.S. Mariposa*, a former Matson luxury liner, now converted to a troopship. Designed for 1200 passengers it now held 6500 GIs; there were 12 of us in a cabin intended for two. We left Boston Harbor on 30 August 1944 to travel the North Atlantic to England unescorted, relying on our speed and frequent zig-zag course changes to outwit any German U-boats. We had to keep totally dark at night and all garbage was dumped overboard just as we changed course.

It is only in retrospect that I can now appreciate the danger of that voyage. While the campaign against the German U-boat wolf packs had been effective, there were still regular sinkings of ships headed across the North Atlantic. We only learned later that two entire combat regiments had been lost when their ships were torpedoed as they headed for the Normandy beaches in the June invasion assault. If the *Mariposa* had taken a German torpedo, that would have been the end of us for there were not enough lifeboats to hold 6,500 of us and a GI in a life jacket in the North Atlantic would not last long. But at the time of our voyage, we tried not think about it very much.

Since the staterooms could accommodate only half the troops, every 48 hours we had to leave our cabin and exchange places with GIs who had been sleeping up on the open deck. That was OK until the damn merchant marine crew started hosing down the deck at 6 am without any warning. You can imagine the panic scene as we had to wake from a sound sleep, leap up, and gather up our blankets and gear to avoid getting them drenched. There we stood, half-dressed, clasping all our belongings to our chest, waiting for the gush of water to subside. We probably looked funny, but it was infuriating. I learned some new words and phrases as our guys reacted to this idiocy.

It was the best kind of voyage — uneventful. On 7 September we steered carefully into Liverpool harbor avoiding all the sunken ships, a grim reminder of the Blitz and a forewarning that we were entering a war zone. This showed us firsthand what the British had endured and a much more sober mood replaced our usual frivolity. A British train took us south and at each stop the English Gray Ladies arrived with tea and scones. Our destination was Falmouth in Cornwall, a charming seaport, where the heroic 29th Division had been billeted before going into Omaha Beach on D-Day. The 29th Division with its blue-and-gray shoulder patch signifying mixed Union and Confederate antecedents fought up through the beach exits and produced a D-Day hero in Gen. Norman Cota, assistant divisional commander.

• • • •

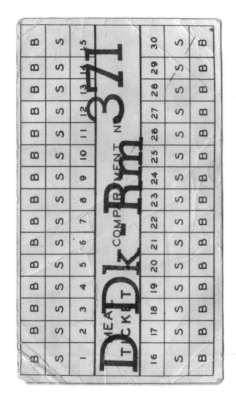

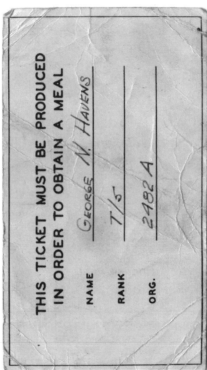

Room pass and meal ticket for cross-Atlantic trip on Mariposa troopship.

CHAPTER TEN

Waiting in Cornwall for Montgomery

We had theorized that the hot, humid, sandy, primitive, remote conditions at Camp Gordon Johnston were to toughen us up for our overseas mission. But no, in Falmouth in another army non sequitur we were quartered in three seashore hotels, the *Holmlea*, *Seabank* and *Primrose*. They overlooked a splendid harbor ringed with palm trees, thanks to the nearness of the warm Gulf Stream, in a location known as the "English Riviera."

Yes, we were jammed 10 in a room for two, we had bunk beds with straw-filled mattresses, there was no central heating, there was a true blackout at night as enemy planes did come over, but they were hotels. Mine was the *Homelea* and we were in a front suite on the ground floor with a fireplace. We wondered what the place had looked like in pre-war England and who had lived in these rooms. Our presence in these hotels revealed the total commitment of the British to the war effort. At any rate it was far better than we had expected, we found the setting along the shore memorable, and some of our guys visited nearby Truro and Penzance. Antiaircraft batteries positioned at each point of the non-commercial harbor fired at the German planes that ventured overhead.

Homelea Hotel, our comfortable quarters in Falmouth, Cornwall, England while waiting for Montgomery to open the Port of Antwerp. (1966 photo)

After we ingeniously hooked up a radio PA system we could tune in and hear the fine Armed Forces Network programs which featured many of the great American big bands. It was a real touch of home for those of us who loved Goodman, Shaw, Ellington and Miller. Further, we could hear the famous British singer, Vera Lynn, on the BBC. She had the songs and the special way of presenting them that stirred our deepest emotions. The best were:

"There'll be bluebirds over the white cliffs of Dover some-day just you wait and see"

"When the lights go on again all over the world"

"Kiss me once and kiss me twice and kiss me once again, it's been a long, long time"

And our favorite, the achingly poignant "We'll meet again, don't know where, don't know when, but I know we'll meet again some sunny day."

Each of us listened to her with the fervent hope that those promises would come true, but we knew that would not be soon.

Our job in blacked-out Falmouth was to work at the US Navy Advance Amphibious Base repairing landing craft — LCMs, LCVPs, LSTs — damaged in the D-Day landings that could be needed for later operations. Our technical guys were in their element, especially when they could cadge some Navy coffee or grub which was far superior to GI fare. Here they unsuccessfully tried to teach me welding and brazing, so I would have a technical skill. But I kept getting the welding rod stuck or burning through the metal with the brazing torch, so I failed that option.

The original logistical plan had us moving quickly to Antwerp to help run the port. But British General Viscount Lord Bernard Law Montgomery failed to move aggressively to dislodge the remaining Germans and open the port. He was too busy dreaming about his forthcoming Market-Garden or "bridge too far" Arnhem operation which became a stunning Allied defeat. So we bided our time in Cornwall.

Four 105th members: (front) Fred Stinnett, Joe Hermann; (rear) Jonathan Ogilvie, Robert Bell in Falmouth. Bell later organized the company's reunions.

Our stay in Falmouth was enjoyable. The city itself was attractive despite the war, and the weather was moderate. Some of our hardiest guys even went swimming in the bay. The under-nourished English kids did their "Any gum, chum" routine and were pathetically grateful for an orange (hadn't had any for five years) or a chocolate bar. I saw my first soccer game and was totally amazed by the endurance that the English lads displayed, doubting that our well-fed, well-trained GIs could have kept up their pace. We walked over into Falmouth town as often as pos-sible to see the sights and sneak some fish and chips which were supposedly off-limits for GIs. Paul Grady had excellent night vision whereas I did not, so on some pitch-black nights as we walked back to our quarters he thought it funny to lose me in the dark of the black-out.

The presence of so many GIs in England produced a mild love-hate relationship. Yes, they were glad to have us there as allies, but some resentments inevitably surfaced. The humorous complaint of the British was that the Americans were "Over-paid, over-sexed and over here!" Proof of the latter was that even in the brief time we were in England, some of our Romeo-type fellow soldiers found cooperative girl friends to enhance their evenings.

The army has a system for everything; it obviates think-ing. One example is the system for assigning GIs to the various job classifications that the army has. And they have a lot. The army requires each new recruit to take the AGCT, the Army Gen-eral Classification Test, which is the basis for selecting his MOS, the Military Occupational Specialty that his aptitudes, abilities, and expertise uniquely qualify him for. The test results are ana-lyzed and MOS assignments made by folks who are either funny, diabolical or insane since one's experience is never matched up to one's MOS classification.

That's why in Falmouth our cooks were mostly former truck drivers, thus the food they served up tasted like it came out of a bad truck stop. I love eggs — scrambled, poached, soft boiled, fried over easy, shirred or omelets — but the eggs they foisted upon us were an insult to the chickens who laid them and we who ate them. One stomach-turning example was powdered eggs that they had scrambled sometime during the night or early morning and left on the steam table till we innocents arrived. By then the eggs were green around the edges of the black pan they resided in. The black pan may have been originally that color or it may have acquired its pernicious patina from too much use and not enough washing. But one thing was clear: the eggs did not like that pan and turned green at the thought of being in it.

On special occasions we were treated to "fresh" eggs although their source was never revealed, perhaps a military secret. You might think that cooking a "fresh" egg is easy, but not when you're used to driving big semis. Our cooks fried the eggs several hours before breakfast, perhaps as a nasty payback for having to get up three hours before their "customers." A lengthy exposure to the heat of a steam table produced a remarkable result, they became more rubbery than Goodyear's best tires. It was almost impossible to stick a fork into one of these eggs and if you dropped one on the floor, it bounced. Our illusions of a breakfast of "fresh" eggs were destroyed as we chewed and chewed in order to swallow these elastic beauties. We thought we saw our cooks smirking over in the corner of the kitchen.

Paul Grady and I led a protest activity against the stupid actions of our then-mess officer, Lt. Robert Rodman. Since the driver-prepared army rations were unappealing, since we had fireplaces in each room, since we had access to some canned foods, we heated them up over the fireplaces during the evening and obviously this food required salt. So salt shakers kept disappearing from the so-called mess hall. This infuriated Rodman, resulting in an unfortunate ultimatum: if any more salt shakers disappear, punishment would ensue. After the next night, guess what, shakers were missing. Rodman could not find the guilty ones so he decreed that until all shakers were returned, all seats would be removed from our mess hall (an idea he must have picked up from Camp Gordon Johnston) and we could eat standing up.

This infuriated Grady and me, so we launched a campaign of "No Seats, No Eats." This is a serious problem since the company must report to higher-ups the number of men fed at each meal. If no one ate, someone from HQ or the IG would appear and start asking embarrassing questions. And, as stated, we had plenty of food in our rooms to tide us over. Our effort was strongly supported, only two guys went through the mess line — the first sergeant (he really had to) and one toady corporal. Grady and I were summoned to the captain's office for a dressing down, but he understood how ludicrous the edict was and canceled it. I heard later that some officers wanted to court martial the two of us and this probably aborted my chances for promotion or any added responsibility in the company. My values for simple justice were something I could not give up.

Enlisted men in a war zone have the letters they send home censored by officers to ensure conformity with secrecy and security regulations. This is another example of the officer-enlisted man class system that I found insulting and degrading (not as bad as the class system in the British army but still infuriating). I found it tough to accept having one of our officers privy to my personal and private thoughts, especially given my critical opinion of their character and leadership capabilities. The reader should understand that I had experienced exemplary leadership with a YMCA executive, summer camp leaders, my infantry platoon leader, my father-in-law, and others. With one or two exceptions our officers came up short and I remained resentful. But one must accept reality, so I wrote regularly to my parents, Ginnie, and friends.

.
.
.

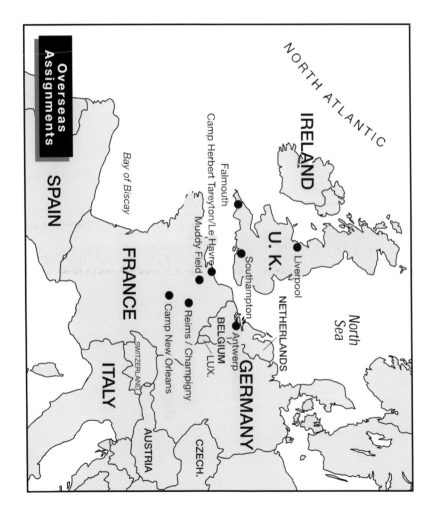

Overseas Assignments: Author's company did vital port marine maintenance work in Falmouth and the Port of Antwerp to keep supplies moving to frontline troops.

Overseas Assignments

NORTH ATLANTIC

IRELAND

U. K.

Liverpool

Falmouth
Camp Herbert Tareyton/Le Havre

Muddy Field

Southampton

NETHERLANDS

North Sea

Bay of Biscay

SPAIN

FRANCE

Reims / Champigny

Camp New Orleans

Antwerp
BELGIUM
LUX.

GERMANY

CZECH.

SWITZERLAND

ITALY

AUSTRIA

CHAPTER ELEVEN

From Le Havre to Antwerp by "40 & 8s"

On 13 November our two-month sojourn in historic Falmouth ended. We entrained for Southampton and boarded a Limey ship, the *Empire Lance*, to take us to France. This was a bad voyage across a choppy Channel on a bad ship with worse food and Limey sailors who were far less than friendly. We got to Le Havre after dark on 15 November and had to debark into an LCT landing craft to get ashore because of the extensive damage to the port facilities. From a 20-foot height we were told to pitch our barracks bags over the side of the ship into the landing craft, not a happy occurrence for those guys who had put various treasured bottles of their favorite beverages in their bags. Then we clambered down the side via rope netting.

Herded into 6x6 trucks we were driven to a rural, muddy field somewhere near historic Agincourt and told to make camp. Grady and I pitched our shelter halves — an useless army contraption developed in the previous century — and still in use! — where it takes the two halves to make a tent but has no floor, has no closure at one end and leaks like a sieve. Wrapping ourselves in our GI blankets we lay down on our raincoats and shivered through the night. It was a cold, damp, muddy, unpleasant week in that field. When it stormed and rained we found a nearby aban-

The "muddy field" near Agincourt in France where we spent a wet, cold, dirty week in November 1944. The army shelter-half tents had no floors and leaked.

doned small building with a fireplace and huddled around it. One night we slept warmly hidden under hay in an adjacent farmer's loft, but were aroused suddenly in early morn as the farmer starting his chores moved toward us with a giant pitchfork. Once again, we reacted swiftly. Later we saw him slaughter and butcher a cow — ugh. One day we were trucked to a facility to take a shower, but when some of our GIs saw the French sign which said "Douche" they panicked and needed some reassuring.

Our maverick company seemed to have a magnetic attraction for weird happenings and the next one was truly unforgettable. On 21 November we were packed into French "40 & 8" box cars originally designed to hold 40 hommes (soldiers) or 8 chevaux (horses). Perhaps they could accommodate 40 smaller French poilus, but 40 GIs — no way! With only 37 of us in our dirty boxcar it was totally impossible for all to get into any kind of sleeping position at night, so a half dozen rode on the roof for awhile, then exchanged with the guys down below.

Our train was headed for Antwerp, normally a day's trip. But with all of the bridges across the Seine below Paris as well as tracks and other railroad facilities bombed out earlier by the Air Force to stymie movement of German forces during the breakout from Normandy, our route was slow and circuitous. We detoured all over northern France and even into Luxembourg. The damage intended to disrupt German defenses ended up disrupting our trip which required three days, not one, arriving on 24 November. I wrote:

At every strategic bridge or switchyard along the way you could see the bomb craters and the repaired tracks. Wrecked German boxcars were everywhere and it was easy to see what the bombing had done to their supply system. We passed through one town...the damage was terrific...houses were shattered and wrecked...devastation was everywhere...it'll take years to rebuild.[12]

Our cars moved slowly, stopped frequently and unpredictably, and started up with no notice other than several high-pitched whistles. When we did stop, guys bailed out of the cramped cars to stretch, scavenge for apples in nearby trees, or run to any close-by house to negotiate for a bottle of calvados or wine. When the whistle sounded, guys came running helter-skelter across fields to catch our car and dive aboard. Several who would not make it simply went to the adjacent highway and hitchhiked to the next village, often beating us there. The car had no toilet, of course, so we had to wait until the train stopped and then take care of our business before the train started up again. Some guys really got caught with their pants down.

Thanksgiving Day 1944 was memorable. Of course the propaganda line back in the States was that it would be a Spartan holiday with "all the turkeys and other goodies sent overseas to our troops." Actually we almost went without any food at all. Only when our Captain Doran demanded that the train commander open up some provisions for us did we get food. Well, it was food, but not what we expected. For each car of 40 GIs we received two round loaves of French farm bread, a gallon can of orange marmalade and a long tin of Spam! Under a barrage of kibitzing about fairness, it became my duty to allocate and serve the food in our car. So I cut each fellow a slice of bread, put on a slice of Spam and covered this with marmalade. That was our Thanksgiving feast. Um-m-m-m.

The next morning we arrived in Antwerp where we would spend the next eight months as a key unit of the 13th Major Port Group, Transportation Corps.

• • • •

CHAPTER TWELVE

. . . .

Antwerp: A Crucial Allied Objective

From D-Day until early September (as we were landing in England) the military situation in the ETO had changed dramatically. After the breakout from the Normandy beachhead in late July and the victory which shattered the German Fifth Panzer and Seventh Armies in the Argentan-Falaise pocket, all of the Allied armies had driven forward with incredible swiftness. By D+98 days they were near the German frontier, a line that the SHAEF planners had not expected to be reached until D+350. That success had its downside in the form of a logistical limitation on further progress.

Each advance moved the troops north and east farther away from their supply bases near the Normandy beaches and Cherbourg, and the increasing remoteness of their supplies started to apply a logistical choke hold. At this time no other channel ports had been captured or opened to receive major shipping. So trucks now had to travel 300 miles and more to deliver their shipments to the frontline divisions, while the 600-mile round trips themselves were consuming gas and tires and wearing out equipment and men. The famous Red Ball Express truck effort delivered supplies to the American armies with an average round trip of 714 miles and took 71 hours. [13]

In the exceptional efforts to solve the transport problem, some divisions were grounded and rendered immobile with their trucks taken from them and used to move supplies.

As Europe's largest peacetime seaport Antwerp, Belgium, was an obvious major strategic target for the Allies to give them a supply port closer to the front lines than the now-remote Normandy beaches and Cherbourg. For the same reason it became a high priority for Hitler to deny its use by the Allies. The capture of Antwerp on 4 September 1944 (D+90) promised to solve the logistical difficulties and it was assumed that the port would be usable about 15 September.

David Kennedy has clearly defined the problem:

An American division in active combat consumed six to seven hundred tons of supplies every day. With some forty divisions in France by early September, and more arriving weekly, the Allies required that at least twenty thousand tons of material move to the front daily from the Channel beaches and their sole functioning port at Cherbourg. The difficulty lay not with the availability of goods. Stocks were still piled high in England, and American farms and factories continued to pour out a deluge of food, guns, and munitions. The problem, rather, was transport.[14]

The obvious solution to the supply bottleneck was the great Port of Antwerp with its extensive facilities able to handle large numbers of ships, its trained dock workers, and its location close to the existing front lines. In his memoirs even Winston Churchill proclaimed the priority of accessing Antwerp:

Eisenhower planned to thrust northeastward in the greatest possible strength and to the utmost limit of his supplies. The main effort was to…take Antwerp. Without the vast harbor of this city no advance across the lower Rhine and into the plains of Northern Germany was possible.[15]

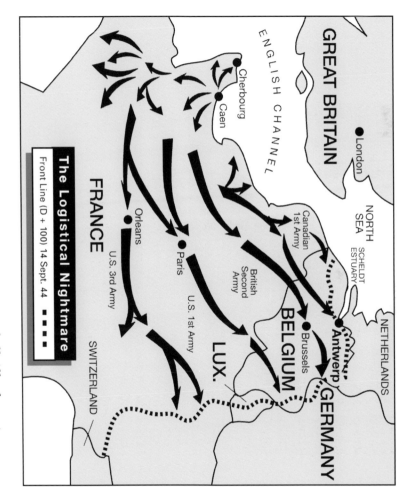

The Logistical Nightmare

Front Line (D + 100) 14 Sept. 44 ▪▪▪▪▪

The Logistical Nightmare: Rapid advance of all Allied armies created long supply lines. British armor raced 250 miles in five days to capture Antwerp unharmed, but then halted.

The Port of Antwerp was the largest in Europe in 1944 and ranked as the third largest seaport in the world. It could be a critical asset for the Allies once it was opened for use and would clearly shorten the war. The Germans well understood

Aerial view of the massive Port of Antwerp. As the largest port in Europe in 1944 it was a prize sought by both the Allies and the Germans.

the value of Antwerp for in their 1941 projected invasion of Britain, it was planned that their Sixteenth Army should embark at Antwerp.

Located some 90 to 100 kilometers up the Scheldt Estuary from the North Sea, Antwerp had a thoroughly sheltered harbor with a minimum depth of eight and a half meters, so that large seagoing vessels could be received at all stages of the tide. Some five and a half kilometers of quays lined the right bank of the Scheldt. Northeast of the city, eighteen wet basins that were reached from the river through four locks provided yet another forty-two kilometers of quays.

The docks were equipped with more than 600 hydraulic and electric cranes, along with many 100-ton and 150-ton floating cranes, loading bridges, and floating grain elevators. In 1938 Antwerp had registered 12,000 sea-going vessels and handled almost 60 million tons of freight.

Its clearance facilities included twelve dry docks, more than 800 kilometers of rails, extensive marshaling yards, and excellent linkage with the Belgian network of over 5,000 kilometers of railroads and 2,200 kilometers of navigable waterways.

When the British 11th Armoured Division rolled into Antwerp on 4 September 1944, German disarray was pervasive. The harbor was almost intact. Almost none of the usual and thorough German demolitions to destroy the port facilities had occurred. Some damage to the locks would preclude immediate usage of the wet basins, three railroad bridges were destroyed, and two sunken coasters and mines would have to be removed from the estuary.

The quays were in good condition, warehouses and sheds mostly intact, and even the port's cranes and other electrical unloading machinery practically untouched and almost all in working order.

For the rest of the war, Hitler would launch repeated efforts to deny the Allies the immense logistical advantage that the Port of Antwerp gave them. He understood all too well that this unique rear-area facility and the supplies that could be unloaded there would now enable the Allies to sustain their offensives into Germany.

The port now is second only to Rotterdam in Europe and the fourth largest in the world handling over 130 million metric tons per year. No other port in Europe is so well equipped for general cargo and it provides jobs for over 57,000 people. Its Berendrecht Lock is the largest in the world measuring 500 meters (547 yards) long by 68 meters (74 yards) wide.[16]

. . . .

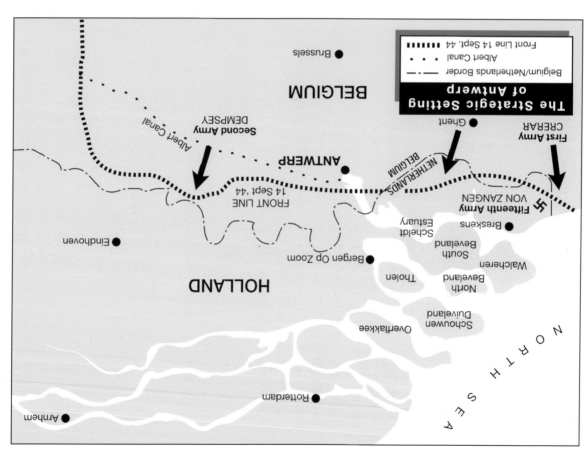

The Strategic Setting of Antwerp: The immense port could not be used until the Germans were driven out of the Breskens Pocket, Scheldt Estuary, Walcheren and South Beveland.

CHAPTER THIRTEEN

The Blunder at Antwerp

Montgomery's British-Canadian 30 Corps under Lt. General B.G. Horrocks captured Antwerp essentially unharmed on 4 September 1944, but then rested and regrouped.

The Germans continued to occupy (1) both banks of the 54-mile stretch of the West Scheldt River leading outward to the North Sea, (2) a sizable area along the North Sea and south of the Scheldt known as the Breskens Pocket, and (3) the Dutch islands of Walcheren and South Beveland near the mouth of the river where there were still V-2 launching sites targeting London. These V-2 batteries did not evacuate the islands until two weeks later as the Allies advanced.[17]

Clearly, no supply ships could move up the Scheldt to Antwerp until the Germans were dislodged and mines removed from the river. Opening the Scheldt River and the port was the crucial objective for Eisenhower to support his fall and winter campaign. "If we can only get to using Antwerp," Eisenhower told Chief of Staff General George C. Marshall, "it will have the effect of a blood transfusion."[18]

The priority to be assigned to the opening of Antwerp quickly became confused in the communications between

Eisenhower and Montgomery, who had other basic disagreements and conflicts on the conduct of the war.

In an order on 29 August 1944 Eisenhower directed Montgomery to take Antwerp…Mindful, however that existing SHAEF contingency plans for Rhine crossings had set as a precondition that Antwerp be in Allied hands and functioning by 15 September 1944, Montgomery had demanded that the U.S. First Army aid him in taking the port…Eisenhower assigned Montgomery the objective, but he did not assign the American troops to assist in taking the objective…The British Chiefs of Staff opposed Montgomery taking Antwerp in the manner ordered…the BCOS questioned the relevance of Antwerp in current operations as well as the idea that Antwerp was a precondition for the (attack on the) Ruhr.[19]

As an alternate to Antwerp, Montgomery had won Eisenhower's reluctant approval to launch his Market-Garden Arnhem offensive to seize the bridges over the lower Rhine as a springboard to move into the key Ruhr area. Launched on 18 September 1944 the daring campaign failed to capture the Arnhem bridge, the "bridge too far," and resulted in an awkward thumb-shaped salient difficult to defend and subject to German counter-attack. The ill-fated operation produced more casualties than the Allies suffered on D-Day. Most important it diverted assets away from the effort to open Antwerp.

At a conference on 22 September, after the Market-Garden defeat:

Eisenhower assigned Montgomery's army group the task of opening Antwerp as a matter of urgent priority. Montgomery's initial neglect of this detail had provoked increasingly frequent reminders from SHAEF of the logistical importance of Antwerp…but as long as Market-Garden might succeed, Eisenhower acquiesced in deferring the Antwerp task out of hope that the war might yet end promptly enough to make the port capacity of Antwerp unnecessary.[20]

We now know that the optimism about an early end to the war was unrealistic and deferring the Antwerp task was a strategic miscalculation which severely aggravated the logistical pinch. Shortly the Allies were to receive a nasty surprise as the resilient, resourceful Germans regrouped and resisted further advances everywhere with great determination. In fact, the war would stretch on for another eight deadly months and account for the bulk of the casualties suffered by the Anglo-American forces in Europe.

As the command confusion persisted, more messages and directives went back and forth until on 27 September Montgomery said that "opening of Antwerp was absolutely essential " but it was still only one of three tasks he gave the First Canadian Army. He ordered them to complete the capture of Calais and Boulogne, develop operations to open Antwerp, and thrust strongly northwards to protect the Second British Army on its west flank (the Arnhem salient).[21]

After Montgomery announced in the 5 October meeting of top SHAEF commanders that he could take the Ruhr without opening Antwerp, Admiral Sir Bertram Ramsey, SHAEF's naval commander-in-chief, wrote in his diary:

This afforded me the cue I needed to lambast him for not having made Antwerp the immediate objective of highest priority, and I let fly with all my guns at the faulty strategy we had allowed. Our large forces were practically grounded for lack of supply, and had we now got Antwerp and not the (Arnhem) corridor we should be in a far better position for launching the knockout blow.[22]

In a memorandum on 8 October Eisenhower's logistical planners who were becoming increasingly anxious about the delay in opening Antwerp, wrote, "The failure to open Antwerp is jeopardizing the soundness of our entire winter campaign."[23]

Then on 9 October Montgomery issued a new directive that "the operations to open Antwerp must have priority." On 16

October Montgomery finally issued a new directive giving unequivocal priority to the opening of Antwerp. This was 42 days after the original capture of the city.

That Montgomery's failure to open the Scheldt may have been deliberate is the opinion of the authors of the authoritative book, *A War to be Won*. He assigned the task to the First Canadian Army but gave it the lowest logistical priority in his 21st Army Group.[24] The long delay was to impose an irrevocable logistical loss to the Allies.

• • • •

CHAPTER FOURTEEN

The Battle for Antwerp

The capture of Antwerp and its port essentially un-harmed on 4 September 1944 was a prize that Allied military planners and generals dreamt of and that must have given Hitler and his generals nightmares.

But the mountains of supplies that could come through the great port to shorten the Allies' lines of supply and shorten the war were at that time just a dream. To make them a reality meant dislodging the Germans from their strongly fortified positions along the 54 miles of the West Scheldt Estuary that led to the North Sea and the formidable positions on Walcheren and South Beveland. No ships could dock, no supplies could be received at Antwerp until that was accomplished.

Two of the major battles in the European Theater were well-reported and are well-known, the "bridge too far" Arnhem offensive and the Battle of the Bulge. But the battle to open the Port of Antwerp was of prime importance and equally decisive.[25] It deserves to be better understood and fully appreciated for its significance.

When the British 11th Armoured Division under Major General G.P.B. Roberts barreled into Antwerp the port facilities were almost intact. They were given splendid assistance by the

Belgian resistance fighters who overwhelmed German engineers, cut key demolition wires and provided accurate intelligence to the British.

But the British neglected to take the key bridges, then undefended, over the Albert Canal on the northern edge of the city. If they had pressed on and driven some 20 miles to the eastern base of the South Beveland peninsula, they could have trapped the remnants of the German Fifteenth Army. General Horrocks's pause to "refit, refuel and rest" until 7 September, even though he had fuel for his tanks, gave the enemy time to dig in and resist with increased tenacity.

Pausing to savor the original triumph at Antwerp had other unhappy results. By not taking the canal bridges and moving aggressively to trap the enemy forces on South Beveland and Walcheren, more than 86,000 men of General Von Zangen's German Fifteenth Army plus 600 artillery pieces, 6,000 vehicles and 6,000 horses were able to escape to southern Holland. This strategic retreat placed them along the west flank of the corridor to Arnhem and contributed to the Allied defeat suffered in the Market-Garden or "bridge too far" Arnhem operation.

Later General Horrocks would admit that "I believe that if we had taken the chance and carried straight on with our advance, instead of halting...the whole course of the war in Europe might have been changed."

General James A. Gavin of the 82nd Airborne Division assessed this oversight:

Liddell Hart in his *History of the Second World War* attributes it to a "multiple lapse - by four commanders from Montgomery downward." And Charles B. MacDonald in his book *The Mighty Endeavor* called the failure "One of the greatest tactical mistakes of the war." I cannot understand how a historian can avoid placing the responsibility on Eisenhower. He, more than anyone else, had a keen awareness of the critical nature of the logistics situation in his armies.[26]

The Germans remained ensconced on both sides of the Scheldt and on South Beveland and Walcheren Islands. On the south bank of the West Scheldt, the German Fifteenth Army held the Breskens Pocket. On the north bank of the West Scheldt were two divisions on Walcheren Island with large fortified gun emplacements and one division on South Beveland.

With some ambiguity Eisenhower assigned Montgomery's army group the task of opening Antwerp to Allied shipping as a matter of urgent priority. Montgomery aggressively refused to tie down more than a bare minimum of his troops and gave the task to the Canadian First Army alone. The polder land terrain with its flooded areas and raised, exposed roads where advancing units were out in the open aided the resolute German defense. The undermanned Canadian army attacked toward South Beveland on 2 October, some 28 days after the fall of Antwerp. After tough fighting under difficult conditions, they destroyed the Breskens Pocket on 21 October. Their first assault on Walcheren on 31 October was repulsed, then finally with bombing of the dikes, an amphibious assault, and the aid of the British 1 Corps resistance on Walcheren ceased on 8 November. This closed this difficult task, a hard and bloody campaign in which casualties exceeded combined Anglo-American losses in Sicily.

The battle to open Antwerp had cost almost 13,000 casualties in the First Canadian Army, the loss of some 40 aircraft, naval losses, and unknown but significant casualties among the Belgian and Dutch Resistance fighters and Belgian and Dutch civilians.

The losses suffered by the Canadians in this bloody engagement seemed especially tragic for several reasons. First is my Canadian heritage, all four of my grandparents and my father were born in Canada. Second was the fact that my cousin, Bill Hodgins, was somewhere with the Canadian Army; I only learned later that he had survived unharmed. Third was our liking and affinity for the Canadian soldiers, Canucks as we called them, whose friendly, happy-go-lucky temperament was more like our American GIs than that of the British soldiers.

Then minesweepers had to clear the length of the Scheldt which was "one of the most difficult and dangerous minesweeping operations of the war." Finally on 26 November the channel was clear after 229 ground mines and 38 moored mines had been removed.[27]

The first Allied ship, the *James B. Weaver*, a Liberty ship reached Antwerp on 28 November just four days after the arrival of our 105th unit. But this was 85 days after Antwerp's capture, which explains why the 105th and our 13th Major Port Group sat in England for two months waiting.

The long delay testified to Montgomery's persistent underestimation of the importance of the port and of the determined strength of the German resistance. The price for Montgomery's distraction with Market-Garden was reckoned not only in lost lives but in the lost opportunity to relieve the supply famine by quickly securing the immense port of Antwerp. Even Montgomery's champion, chief of the British Imperial General Staff General Alan Brooke, felt that "Monty's strategy for once is at fault. Instead of carrying out the advance on Arnhem he ought to have made certain of Antwerp in the first place." For a fuller treatment of this fiasco, see *A War to be Won*[28] and *Eisenhower at War*.[29]

Once again we are made to understand that there is no combat power without good logistics. A successful army needs both strong frontline fighters and capable rear-area service support. That is what makes for good headlines.

. . .

Doing the Job in Antwerp

In Antwerp we were stationed on the third floor of Building 5 in Luchtbal Barracks on the north side of the city between Eekeren and Merxem, not far from the Dutch border, along with some 3,000 other GIs. It was a rather grim, brick complex with nothing to relieve its exterior visual drabness, but it did have a chapel, theater, PX and hot showers. We were quartered 30 men

Entrance to the grim Luchtbal Barracks in Antwerp, home to 3000 GIs, "buzz bomb" chicken and the 105th.

in a room equipped with double bunks that had no mattresses; we slept on wooden slats softened only by a blanket. With a situation far better than that of the frontline troops, we had no serious complaints, just the ordinary army gripes.

This facility was built for Belgian army troops, but after the 1940 German blitzkreig it was occupied by the Wehrmacht soldiers who painted their ugly swastikas, slogans and banners on the squad room walls. When we moved in, we painted over them and put up pin-up pictures of Betty Grable, Ann Sheridan, Lana Turner and other beauties — a telling differentiation in the cultures of the two armies.

As soon as we occupied the Luchtbal Barracks we learned that it was close to the dock area and thus in the target area for the German V-weapons, Hitler's next effort to disrupt port operations. Even though we were a rear-area support company we

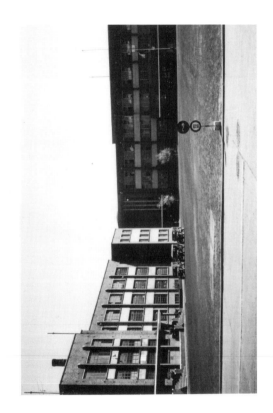

Interior parade ground of Luchtbal Barracks once occupied by the victorious German Wehrmacht army from 1940 to 1944. (1966 photo)

quickly understood that we would be in the line of fire.

Our mission was to help open, operate and maintain the port facilities including keeping the essential harbor craft vessels operational. These included fire boats, tugs, sea mules, huge 100-ton capacity floating cranes which could lift tanks and locomotives off of the ships, and many types of military craft. We did this from our operational base in the port at Docks 289 and 291 where we constructed complete repair shop facilities.

We repaired or replaced marine engines, serviced diesel engine injectors, changed drive shafts and propellers, installed new equipment, repaired hoisting cables and other crane equipment, did preventive maintenance, corrected damage to these vessels incurred by bombs or accidents, and performed underwater work with our divers. When the Gray Marine diesel engines on the MT boats frequently failed and could not be repaired due to parts shortages, Arthur G. Moore of the 105th developed an innovative technique to replace them with available Chrysler Royal marine engines so that the MTs could keep running. When replacement parts for various vessels were not to be found, technicians

View of cranes, tugs and other harbor craft in the Port of Antwerp that were maintained by the 105th to keep supplies moving.

from the 105th created ingenious ways to make new parts. When a fierce January storm created havoc in the port, we recovered and repaired many small boats and other equipment that had been tossed about by wind and waves. When we needed larger machinery or tools than we possessed, we worked closely with the Port's Belgian machinists. Lt. Roy Stephens who supervised much of the 105th's work in the Port commented, "We worked on a bunch of the LCM landing craft which were later used by combat divisions to hop the Rhine River."

Among the facilities at the Port were extensive Belgian marine engineering and ship-repairing workshops with modern, massive machinery. Much of this machinery had become rusted and unusable due to disuse and exposure to the elements from bomb damage to the buildings. We assisted the Belgians in removing protective structures from the machinery, cleaning them and returning them to productive use so the Port could get its postwar commerce going again.

Although the records of the 105th are not complete for our first months in Antwerp, they do show that we completed 61 repair jobs in March, 84 in April and 107 in May 1945. Initially we worked every day with only Sunday morning off for religious services; later we were given one day off a week.

The good lieutenant, Roy L. Stephens Jr. of Gig Harbor, Washington, was a standout among the officers and worked with the author on orientation programs.

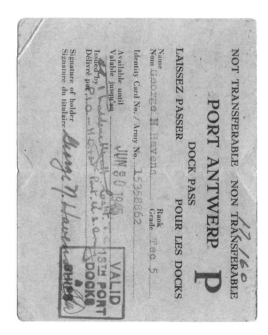

Author's dock pass required for admission to the Port of Antwerp with its invaluable mountains of supplies.

While there were thousands of British soldiers, American GIs and Belgian civilians involved in this mammoth supply effort, we played our part in the record of this great port where half of everything that came to Europe by ship came to Antwerp. We performed a vital role — working on hundreds of boats and the cranes to keep them running so supplies could keep moving to the frontline troops.

Before the port was opened Eisenhower decided that the port should be operated under British control with a defined sector of the facility allocated to the Americans. The American sector was supervised by the 13th Major Port Group, which had been in Falmouth and Plymouth, and the 5th Major Port Group coming in from Brittany.

The opening of Antwerp "effected nothing less than a complete revolution in the supply position of the Allied armies." Within a few weeks Antwerp had all but replaced the long and troublesome line of supply to Cherbourg. By the end of December daily unloadings were 13,700 tons for the Americans and 8,600 tons for the British. That rate steadily increased until by the end of April the Americans alone were discharging 25,000 tons daily. Total imports into northwest Europe estimated at 2 million tons a month in November jumped to 3 million tons monthly in April (which includes tonnage received at secondary channel ports).[30]

The Stars and Stripes 11 November 1944

The following data shows the enormous surge of supplies which flowed into and through the Port of Antwerp during the period 28 November 1944 to 15 December 1945:[31]

Discharged from British ships:

Military Supplies	3,095,996 tons
P.O.L.	225,912 tons
Bulk P.O.L.	2,517,517 tons

Discharged from American ships:

Military Supplies	4,057,907 tons
Bulk P.O.L.	974,278 tons
Bulk oil	94,084 tons

Total Discharged   11,019,694 tons

Note: P.O.L. = Petrol (gas) Oil and Lubricants

The detailed data in Appendix A shows the growing number of vessels and tonnage unloaded at the Port:

Month		Ships	Tonnage
December	1944	160	452,103
January	1945	166	499,156
February	1945	155	430,391
March	1945	220	670,980
April	1945	219	742,086
May	1945	182	762,317
	— War ends —		
June	1945	142	555,117
July	1945	108	437,269

Note: The decline in February was the result of the Battle of the Bulge which disrupted schedules, deferred movement of supplies to threatened bases at Liege and Namur, and backed up ships with cargoes waiting to be unloaded.

This flood of supplies sustained the Allied drives into Germany and met the additional needs of liberated and occupied countries, the liberated Allied POWs, and the large numbers of German POWs. And, of course, it enabled the positive headlines that appeared in the newspapers.

Even after its opening the Germans expended persistent efforts, in addition to the aerial and V-weapon attacks, to restrict the Port's use including air mining of the estuary where a sunken ship could block access to the port for many days. In addition:

At sea 50 (German) E-boats...made forays at night seeking to intercept convoys bound for Antwerp. Some 26 Seehund two-man submarines were sent to attack shipping in the sea approaches, and a number of the 140 one-man midgets tried to reach the estuary.[32]

On a single day the E-boats and U-boats prowling the entrance to the Scheldt torpedoed four American merchant ships sinking three while the fourth was beached and unloaded. A special sabotage swimmer reached and blew up a gate of the vital Kruisschans Locks which controlled the water level in the port. German ME 262 jets bombed warehouses and ships, including a bomb that was dropped into the hold of the *Alcoa Banner* as it was being unloaded.[33] This unrelenting campaign to attack the port attested to its criticality in the Allied efforts to win the logistical war.

U.S. Army Enlisted Ranks: World War II

Insignia for both arms

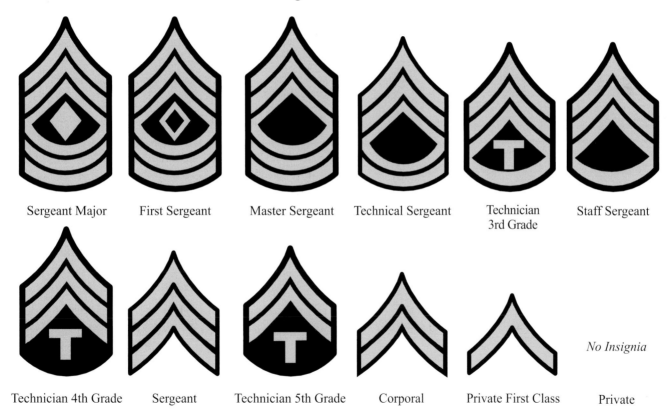

| Sergeant Major | First Sergeant | Master Sergeant | Technical Sergeant | Technician 3rd Grade | Staff Sergeant |

| Technician 4th Grade | Sergeant | Technician 5th Grade | Corporal | Private First Class | Private |

No Insignia

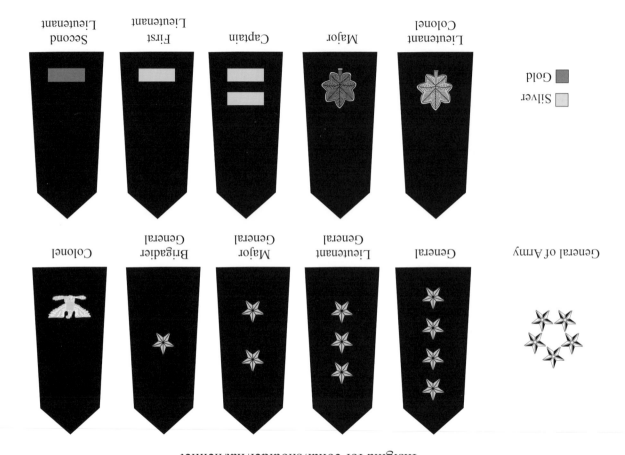

U.S. Army Officer Ranks: World War II

Insignia for collar/shoulder/hat/helmet

Silver
Gold

Second Lieutenant
First Lieutenant
Captain
Major
Lieutenant Colonel

Colonel
Brigadier General
Major General
Lieutenant General
General
General of Army

• • • • • • •

CHAPTER SIXTEEN

V-bombs and No Way to Shoot Back

On 13 June 1944, a week after D-Day, Hitler launched the first V-1 bomb against England and initiated a new form of warfare.

The V-bombs, known as the V-1 and the V-2, were called revenge weapons with the V shortened from the German word, Vergeltungswaffen. They were intended to be

A German V-1 "buzz bomb" in flight over Antwerp. Over 4,800 of these revenge weapons bombarded the city and its port causing death and destruction.

Hitler's revenge for the night bombings of Hamburg, Dresden and other German cities by the Royal Air Force. The V-weapon assault was a new tactic in warfare in which the Germans might never know whether they had hit or missed their target. It was a nameless, faceless horror simply delivering high explosives via crude aiming devices. It was contemplated that a months-long, day-and-night campaign against the British would create panic and disorganization, and contribute to ending the war.[34]

Initially cool to the concept, Hitler later became enamored of the unmanned V-weapons and chose to build them in preference to additional fighter planes where a limiting factor to aircraft use was the shortage of trained pilots. Estimated total production of these new weapons was 6,000 V-2s and 22,400 of the cheaper V-1s, the production equivalent of 24,000 planes during the last two years of the war.[35]

The Luftwaffe-developed V-1 was an early cruise missile, an unmanned robot launched from a fixed catapult ramp, powered by a pulsejet engine, with a crude timing device intended to shut off over the target so that it would then dive to the ground. At the conclusion of its terminal dive the high-explosive charge in its nose, just under one ton, detonated causing extensive damage. While some have referred to it as an "aerial torpedo," its loud distinctive engine noise earned it the nickname of "buzz bomb." Thus it was both a destructive and a psychological weapon.

Defending against the 400-mile-per-hour V-1 cruise missile was difficult. It was too fast for Spitfire or Mustang fighter planes to catch and was a tough target for antiaircraft batteries. Early in our Antwerp days we would watch the V-1s being launched from their ramps just beyond the front lines in southern Holland only some 50 miles away. The ack-ack gunners tried hard but could knock down only a small fraction of the V-1s, usually three or four out of 20. Later when they got the proximity fuse for their shells, their kill ratio jumped sharply.

The V-2 was different, it was a stealth weapon as described by David Kennedy:

The V-2 was a far more sophisticated weapon than the V-1, a true rocket powered by a liquid-oxygen-fueled jet engine that lofted the missile to an altitude of sixty miles and aimed it earthward in a free-fall of 2,200 miles per hour. The V-2 out-ran its own sound waves, exploding without any warning of its arrival. At that speed it was incapable of interception by antiaircraft or fighter interceptors.[36]

The birth of the V-2 dates back to 1929-30 when German liquid-fuel rocket development began in earnest. By 1936 various designs had progressed under the leadership of Wernher Von Braun and others, culminating in the A-4 model, the one ultimately used for quantity production. It was designed in detail in 1939-41 with a 56,000-lb thrust engine and a 2,200-lb warhead of which three quarters were explosives. It was 46 feet long and 5.42 feet in diameter with a nominal range of 156 miles. Some 6,000 were built and 3,200 fired at enemy targets. It was a true ballistic missile which in postwar America, again under Von Braun's leadership, provided the basic technology for our Redstone and Saturn missiles. Despite Von Braun's work for the U.S. at our Huntsville (Alabama) Redstone Arsenal, it should be remembered that he was an SS Nazi officer and concurred in the use of slave labor to build the A-4s.[37]

Since the initial German effort of fortifying the Scheldt Estuary to prevent the opening the port had failed, the Nazis launched their next endeavor to halt port operations, a six-month barrage of their secret revenge weapons, the V-1 buzz bomb and V-2 rocket bomb. A total of 5,960 V-bombs landed in Antwerp and arrondissement starting on 7 October 1944 and ending on 30 March 1945, a daily average of 34 incidents.

Most people associate the V-bomb attacks with London and the well-publicized damage to that city. But the stalwart, stoic British could never be demoralized by V-bombs and Antwerp was the more important strategic target and much closer to the German launching sites in southern Holland. In fact, while London got the publicity, Antwerp got more V-bombs, several times as many as the English capital. Stephen Ambrose in *D-Day: June 6, 1944* reports:

But Hitler was eager to hit London...He had a weapon to do it with, the V-1. It had been flown successfully on Christmas Eve 1943; by June 1944 it was almost ready to go to work. The V-1 was a jet-powered plane (unmanned) carrying a one-ton arhead. It was wildly inaccurate (of the 8,000 launched against London, only 20% even hit that huge target).[38]

Author Norman Gelb estimates that perhaps 2,500 V-1 "buzz bombs" fell on London.[39] Another source reports that some 1,610 V-2s hit Antwerp vs. some 1358 in London.[40] And a well-regarded World War II historian states "more V-2s were eventually fired at the Belgian port of Antwerp than at London."[41]

Captured German V-1 "buzz bomb" on display in Antwerp after V-E Day.

Some of the early V-2 launches were targeted at Paris, Lille, and other cities, but after 12 October the only targets were Antwerp and London. By 31 December 1944 the rocket batteries had fired a total of 1561 V-2s—447 against London, 924 against Antwerp.[42]

A total of 150 V-1s and 152 V-2s hit and exploded in the dock area, including one V-2 close to our 105th repair shops.

They sank two large ships and 58 smaller ones, damaged the Kruisschans Lock, although only enough to slow its working, and twice hit the Hoboken petrol installations.[43]

Captured German V-2 rocket bomb, a true ballistic stealth missile on display.

But the V-bombs did not halt the round-the-clock port operations and immense credit goes to the courageous Belgian dock workers, some 12,000 of them in the American sector alone, who stayed on the job and defied the danger. They sent their families to Brussels or the countryside, then came to work each day tromping down the cobblestone streets to the docks in their wooden shoes: known as *klomps* in Dutch or *sabots* in French.

They were irreplaceable stalwarts because we did not have the manpower to do the job without them. Tragically, 131 of these port employees were killed doing their job.[44] And they did do their job as eventually, more supplies were brought in through Antwerp than all other Allied ports combined.

An expert on physiology has concluded that the impact of terrorism varies with three factors: novelty, sense of helplessness, and lack of warning.[45] He notes that "new forms of terrorism are most frightening in their first use, when the targeted population is unprepared psychologically as well as physically." Clearly, Antwerp civilians and Allied soldiers were not prepared for this frightening new weapon. They were totally defenseless against the V-2 rocket missiles where there was zero warning, just the enormous impact explosions, which must be feared constantly. Further, they were basically helpless against the noisy V-1 buzz bombs that got through the antiaircraft defenses. With the V-1 the warning was the dreaded sound of the pulsejet engine and then its cutoff prior to its descent into Antwerp.

As long as you could hear the loud engine, you were safe. But when it cut off, you knew the V-1 was diving toward Antwerp to destroy whatever it hit. If it cut off overhead, you dove for any cover possible. The constant barrage of V-1s, the frightening engine noise, and the unpredictability of the cut off made us jumpy, nervous, and paranoid. There was no quiet time, there was no real shelter, there was no escape, there was no way to shoot back — just suck it up, keep on going and take it. In fact, when front line soldiers were rotated to Antwerp for MP duty or R&R, they refused to stay because of the constant terror.

On a clear day we could sometimes see the V-2's launch plume in the far distance and we knew that in several minutes a V-2 would land somewhere in Antwerp. And it was a one-way battle since we had no way to counterattack or fight back. The V-bomb barrage would stop only when their launch sites had been overrun by our advancing troops or their production and transportation facilities destroyed by bombing. Bombing of the launch sites was not effective as the V-1 launch ramps were portable and could be easily moved while the V-2 sites were well-protected by German antiaircraft batteries.

V-bombs had a psychological as well as explosive impact on those of us in the target zone. We all had the jitters and were startled and unnerved by a truck backfire or other loud noise. In my case after some months of constant exposure to them, I started to stutter, the only time in my life this has ever happened. I attribute this to the unrelieved stress and strain of the V-bombs and their random unpredictability. As with all stutterers I had trouble pronouncing the soft sounds, in one instance I recall I could not get out the name of the opera singer, Lily Pons. This affliction was temporary and disappeared with the end of the V-bomb barrage.

The official V-bomb attack record in Appendix B shows that Antwerp endured 4,248 V-1 impacts plus 1,712 V-2s, a total of 5,960 incidents. These new weapons produced thousands of civilian and military casualties as well as extensive damage to homes, buildings, the Torengebouw skyscraper, the Rex Cinema, the Ghent railroad tunnel, the Institute for Christian Education, a military hospital, port facilities and ships.

There were many serious incidents. Immediately after our arrival in Antwerp on 27 November 1944 a V-2 hit the busy main downtown intersection of the Frankriklei near the Keizerlei just before noon killing 128 civilians and 26 Allied soldiers while injuring 196 civilians and 113 soldiers.[46]

At 13.30 hours on 19 February 1945, a V-1 that had been wounded and knocked off course by a proximity shell roared into our nearby motor pool at Luchtbal. Along with others from our work crew I was in the barracks for a moment before heading out for afternoon assignments. I was in an upper bunk and dove to get under the bunk, but landed on a buddy who had been in a lower bunk. With the loudest noise I ever hope to hear, its blast impacted the company next to us killing 12 GIs. It blew in all of our windows causing numerous flying glass injuries to our guys with debris all over the bunk room. We survived without fatalities in our company but lost any

Damage caused by a V-1 bomb that hit the motor pool adjacent to our quarters in Luchtbal Barracks on 19 February 1945 killing 12 persons.

outside light in our bunk room since we had to board up the windows to keep out the winter cold.

Shortly after that incident, a V-2 rocket bomb hit about 75 yards from our dockside facility creating an immense crater but no injuries since no one was nearby.

In the terrible Rex Cinema disaster of Saturday 16 December a V-2 hit the crowded theater at 15.15 hours causing the deaths of 296 Allied soldiers and 271 civilians and injuries to 291 others. It was the worst Allied loss of life from a single bomb in the entire war.[47] Two of our 105th guys were buying tickets to enter the theater when the V-bomb hit; they were knocked flat but otherwise unhurt. Rescue crews removed all living persons by the morning of the 19th and all bodies were removed in six days. Immediately after this incident, all public gatherings at events and performances in Antwerp were banned.

Frank Connors and Jonathan Ogilvie in dress uniforms ready for a trip into Antwerp where they narrowly escaped being casualties in the Rex Cinema disaster.

Interior of the Rex Cinema which was hit by a V-2 rocket on 16 December 1944 causing 567 deaths, the worst Allied bombing disaster of the war.

Ultimately, 2,000 buildings were destroyed in Antwerp. Nearly 5,000 were damaged beyond hope of repair, nearly 15,000 needed major repairs, and more than 45,000 required minor repairs. The barrage resulted in 63% of the city's buildings being damaged or destroyed.[48]

Rescue workers dig through the rubble caused by a V-weapon explosion in Antwerp.

V-weapons damaged or destroyed over half of the buildings in Antwerp. Note water-filled crater in foreground where bomb hit.

Russell F. Weigley emphasizes that throughout the war Hitler maintained his fanatical conception of absolutely vital areas not to be relinquished. As a result the Western Front bent awkwardly and lengthily westward at its northern end so that much of Holland could be retained to launch V-bombs. Hitler still hoped to close the Port of Antwerp, though months of such attacks had long since demonstrated their futility for any purpose beyond killing and maiming Belgian civilians and Allied soldiers.[49]

• • •

CHAPTER SEVENTEEN

Luchtbal Barracks and "Buzz Bomb" Chicken

Life in Luchtbal Barracks had its bizarre and weirdly humorous aspects. Let's start with the food which was served to over 3,000 GIs in a consolidated mess — that's the army term for a kitchen that serves multiple companies but, to be clear, it was a consolidated *mess*! One favorite dish was supposed to be chicken ala king, but when ladled into our mess kits it included not only meat but strange chicken parts, bones, gristle, feathers and who knows what else. It quickly earned the marvelous name of "Buzz Bomb Chicken" — the allusion being that a buzz bomb had landed somewhere in a chicken yard and they had simply scooped everything that resulted and dumped it into the pot.

Another bad memory was stew. This may be one of your favorite dishes but it was not the version we were served. As we went through the mess line, the cooks were lined up behind big metal pots where the only thing visible in the pots was grease. They plunged their ladles down into the grease, came up with unknown solid material and dumped it into our mess kits. This produced an uncanny but unavoidable result for many guys four hours later — the "GIs" or severe, unhappy cramps and diarrhea. With our squad room on the third floor we had to go down to the ground floor and cross 60 feet outside to a separate building with a series of toilets designed by a sadistic indi-

Result of Luchtbal's infamous chow — a frantic race to the outdoor latrine with the GI "trots."

vidual. They were open to the air in a severe Belgian winter. They had no wooden seats, just porcelain to sit on. There were no lights or flushing mechanism. They would have been unacceptable even in the Dark Ages and I've seen far better facilities in 2000-year old Roman forts. Still it was humorous, in a strange army way, when about 10 pm you'd hear guys leap from their bunks, hit the floor running, and race for our "outside head" hoping to find an open stall. One person, Leslie Haun, would be so badly distressed that he would not come back upstairs to the bunkroom, instead he would stand inside the first floor barracks door by a radiator and wait for the next of several attacks. The ultimate oxymoron is "army food."

That same Leslie Haun, who had been in the Civilian Conservation Corps (CCC) during the '30s, was a tall, gangly guy whose feet stuck out over the end of his upper bunk. But

*The author in work
fatigues on the docks
near 105th repair shops
in the Port of Antwerp.*

what was spectacular about him was that he slept with his eyes open — his eyeballs rolled down but his eyelids stayed up creating a bizarre scene. We had fun with a visitor or a new recruit as we asked them if they wanted to see the dead guy in our bunkroom, that he had been sick but now we thought he was dead. His appearance really spooked them and they could not leave fast enough. Haun never woke up through all this.

Without the skills or interest to be a welder or steamfitter, I was designated as the Information & Education Non-com for the company a function required by Supreme Headquarters Allied Expeditionary Forces (SHAEF). One of my duties was to create and publish the daily company newspaper, *The 105th News* (at our 50th company reunion in 1994 in Daytona Beach, Florida I was given a complete bound set of the 80 issues, a very special remembrance to me). Up-to-date facts on the war were obtained each morning from a BBC broadcast of the news at dictation speed. Then I used our state-of-the-art equipment — a manual typewriter, a stencil, and a hand-cranked Mimeograph machine — to publish the issues. It was distributed to the men at noon. The paper kept everyone briefed on the progress of the war, alerted them on new company policies and assignments, squelched rumors and scuttlebutt, even included some raunchy humor, and clearly had a positive effect on morale. The 105th was probably one of the few outfits of its size to have a daily newspaper, which was to the credit of the company commander.

I conducted weekly orientation sessions for the company on the war situation, our allies, redeployment and similar topics as I regained some of my public speaking skills honed in those high school debates. Further I supervised the company library, maintained battle situation maps, wrote the monthly company histories, and planned company social events. We held three raucous parties (one a V-E Day celebration) at the Magic Palace facility in Antwerp with Belgique girls, an American band, dancing, and lots of beer plus more serious beverages which were smuggled in by our guys. Getting our company to party was like striking a match to gasoline — they just took off and never quit. It was all for morale, you see.

But mostly I was on Sgt. Charlie Gerlinger's work crew where we did just about any jobs no one else wanted to do to

Sgt. Charlie Gerlinger's work crew in Antwerp: (Clockwise from front) Bill Powers, the author; Oscar Price, Walter Bennett, Gerlinger, Donald Lobb.

A dirty, hard-working trio of Oscar Price, Harold Pfeffer and the author in the Antwerp dock area, Spring 1945.

support our company's mission. Typically we were riding around in open trucks hauling materiel and doing various dirty work like changing the huge, long, heavy, oil-soaked, winch cables on a 100-ton crane in freezing weather. That little endeavor took all night and part of the next morning after we had worked all the previous day, that's over 27 hours straight. Somehow our officers could not find anybody else to relieve our unhappy crew as we fumbled with frozen fingers and exhausted bodies to complete this vital task, which we did. Then that vital crane could resume lifting tanks, howitzers and other heavy equipment off the incoming supply ships.

• • • • •

CHAPTER EIGHTEEN

Von Rundstedt Aims at Antwerp

Our company had just settled into its Antwerp routine when all hell broke loose on 16 December 1944, with the news of the German attack through the Ardennes, later known as "the Battle of the Bulge." This was Hitler's third effort to nullify the use of the Port of Antwerp by the Allies.

First, the Germans fortified the Scheldt River as well as Walcheren and South Beveland Islands to create an 85-day delay. Second, the V-bomb attack while devastating did not halt port operations. So now the Fuhrer ordered Field Marshall Gerd von Rundstedt with three armies to break through, drive 100 miles to capture Antwerp, seize the mountains of supplies there, split the American and British forces, and change the outcome of the war:

Antwerp, already under constant V-bomb bombardment, was the prize. With the great port again in German hands, the Allied supply famine would starve the Allies to a halt in the west. A full-scale V-weapon blitz could then be launched against England. And the Anglo-Americans might yet be forced into a negotiated peace, freeing the Wehrmacht for a last-ditch defense against the relentlessly oncoming Russians.[50]

It is worth noting that this major offensive underscored the strategic value of the rear area and its logistics: the great port, its infrastructure, its treasure of critical supplies and its technically trained personnel.

"War is mainly a catalogue of blunders," Winston Churchill observed in his memoirs. But the Allied failure to anticipate this offensive or discover the preparations for the attack

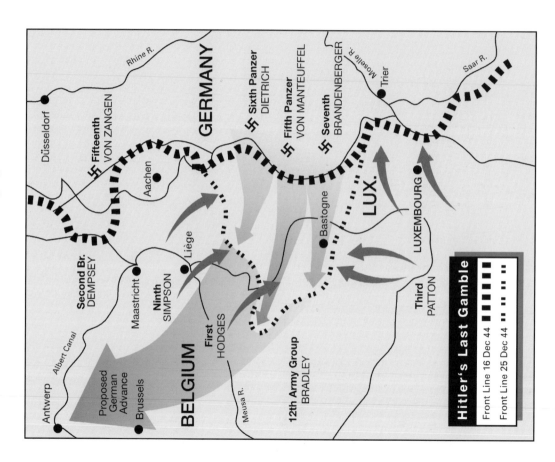

Hitler's Last Gamble: Surprise Ardennes offensive, Battle of the Bulge, was designed to reach Antwerp, seize the supplies, split the Allied armies, and change the war's outcome.

was a monumental failure of SHAEF intelligence. Carlo D'Este in *Patton: A Genius for War* comments:

> General Patton's G-2 intelligence officer, Oscar Koch, was the only Allied intelligence officer to anticipate trouble and plan on how to deal with it. Thus, where other intelligence officers were lulling their commanders with false optimism and wishful thinking that nothing serious was imminent, the Third Army made plans to deal with what no one else believed would occur.[51]

The reaction at our 13th Major Port Headquarters to the imminent prospect of German SS Oberstgruppenfuhrer "Sepp" Dietrich's Sixth Panzer Army, the designated spearhead, breaking through and arriving in Antwerp was panic. I was sent to Port HQ as liaison from our company to receive and relay any orders, and the scene was bizarre with majors and colonels running around like chickens with their heads cut off.

Our company situation changed abruptly as defense not logistics became the priority dictated by the German offensive. What confronted us was that Antwerp was the obvious target, enemy paratroop infiltrators in American uniforms had reportedly been dropped in our area, and the port and its supplies were at risk.

Even though the 105th was a non-combat outfit we were ordered to take up defensive positions to help protect the port with the friendly, reassuring statement that "there will be no retreat, you are expendable." Captain Doran quickly reorganized our company into combat platoons, now headed up by Grady, myself and others with infantry training. We marched out to our assigned positions, waited, and watched for any German infiltrators who might show up in GI uniforms. This was serious business, the real stuff with outposts, passwords and live ammunition in our carbines, but some of our men did not understand what was at stake. One who approached my position in the dark did not remember the password and I had the safety off and my finger on the trigger of my carbine when I finally recognized him.

This defensive perimeter activity continued for several days until it became clear that the German offensive had been blunted, and then was stopped at Bastogne by the magnificent defense of the 101st Airborne Division, and General Patton who had ridden to the rescue with three divisions of his Third Army. By mid-January the "Bulge" was over but the V-bombs continued unabated until 30 March 1945.

Turning point in the Battle of the Bulge: Patton's Third Army relieves Bastogne and launches new drive into German flank.

Copyright © 1945 by the New York Times Co. Reprinted by permission.

One of those who made the headlines as a stalwart hero of the Bulge was Brig. General William M. Hoge who led Combat Command B of the 9th Armored Division in its fearless defense of the St. Vith sector of the battle. Later on 7 March 1945 he had the distinction of capturing the Ludendorff Bridge at Remagen, Germany, the first Allied crossing of the Rhine River. He was then promoted to command of the 4th Armored Division in Patton's Third Army. After WW II he retired from the army, served as chairman of a Cleveland corporation, and lived near our home in the Forest Hill section of East Cleveland. A quiet,

The Stars and Stripes 28 April 1945

diffident individual he was a guest in our home for dinner during the '60s, a special treat for a former first sergeant.

In early April with some skepticism and continuing paranoia we started to believe that the V-bomb barrage had ceased. In fact, Antwerp could no longer be the German's target of choice as the V-1 and V-2 launch sites had been overrun by Allied troops and captured. Slowly, we started to relax and stop listening for the next buzz bomb, finally accepting that our ordeal was over. Later that month, the Antwerp blackout was lifted and life seeped back into the battered city.

On 28 April 1945 the members of the 105th were awarded battle credit for participation in the campaign "Germany" entitling them to wear a bronze battle star.

· · · ·

CHAPTER NINETEEN

The War Winds Down

. . . .

The Stars and Stripes 5 May 1945

Antwerp is the second largest city in Belgium (after Brussels, the capital) with over a quarter million residents, a major seaport city with the typical attractions desired by sailors. It is located in Flanders, the northern Flemish part of Belgium, close to the border with The Netherlands. The official language is Dutch, but most people speak several languages fluently including English so there was little opportunity to learn their language.

It is helpful to know that Belgium is divided into a Flemish-speaking population in the north where Antwerp is located and a French-speaking Walloon section in the south. Indeed, in English it is *Antwerp*, but in Dutch it's *Antwerpen*, and in French it's *Anvers*.

Antwerp is a modern commercial, industrial and financial center linked with the industry in eastern Belgium by the Albert Canal. It is a focal center of the international diamond trade and is the seat of the world's first stock exchange dating to 1460. The painters Quentin Massys and P.R. Rubens resided in the city and Anthony van Dyke was born there.

What are my memories of this city? It had busy, over-crowded trams where you uttered "Alstublieft" (Dutch for "Please") to gain access or to exit. A vast sprawling dock area teeming with Allied shipping. A modern city center with a splendid Gothic Cathedral of Notre Dame, a Renaissance-style city hall, Rubens's house, the guildhalls lining the Groote Markt, sky-scraper, opera house, train station, museums, bars, restaurants, and the historic Steen fortification along the Scheldt. Here was an artist who sketched a superb portrait of Ginnie from a small wallet picture for the popular black market exchange medium of that time, a carton of cigarettes. From here I sent home wooden shoes, lace handkerchiefs, fragments of V-bombs, and other memorabilia to Mom, Ginnie and my sister. And we could get day passes to visit Brussels; the fast electric train took less than an hour to reach the handsome city we called "the little Paris" some 28 miles away.

Some incidents are etched indelibly in my memory. After V-E Day I saw trains arrive at the railroad station from the slave labor camps in Germany. The cars were jammed, crammed and overloaded with poorly clothed, half starved men who had spent months or years in Nazi camps, mines or factories and were now returning home. The station was packed with emotional, desperate relatives eagerly searching for a husband, brother or son. It was a truly heart-rending situation and I felt embarrassed to be observing such an open display of extremely personal feelings.

The Rex Cinema disaster had stopped all large public gatherings, but now after V-E Day the lights came back on and Antwerp slowly re-established its civic life. We learned that the Royal Flemish Opera (Koninklijke Vlaamsche Opera in Dutch)

The Stars and Stripes 2 May 1945

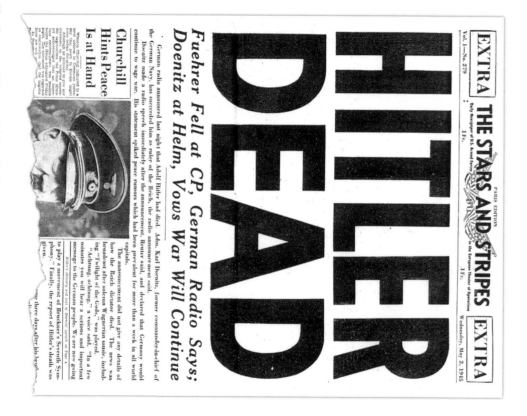

would re-open quickly with "Carmen" and our college gang decided to go. I'm not sure how professional the performance was but they sure deserved great credit for the effort. During the opera written by Bizet in French an amusing gaffe occurred when a singer who was supposed to say "Sil vous plait" in French slipped and intoned "Alstublieft" in Dutch. Our involuntary laughs were quickly hushed by proud Antwerp folks nearby.

As the Information & Education Non-com for the 105th I got to work with our best officer, Lt. Roy Stephens. With Allied forces pushing deep into Germany in 1945, the end of the war was imminent. The I&E activity had been created to deal with the problem of millions of GIs who would necessarily remain in the post-war ETO for many months until shipping was available to take them home or to the Pacific Theater. The army's notion

To learn how to conduct information and education programs Lt. Roy Stephens (second from left) and the author (extreme right) attended an army school in Lille, France.

was that the situation required a comprehensive program of educational courses, entertainment and orientation to sustain the morale of the troops; more close order drill and busy-work activities would not do the job. Stephens and I were sent to Lille, France, to an Army I&E three-day short course on planning and developing these programs. My only memory is hearing the song "Don't Fence Me In" with the first line that goes "Oh Give Me Land, Lotsa Land" for the first time.

Just before V-E Day I was sent to Cite Universitaire in Paris for a five-day I&E course. This is where the foreign students attending the Sorbonne lived and I was coincidentally housed in the Belgian House. The highlight of that experience was on the afternoon of the last day when Gertrude Stein visited our classroom and talked with us for perhaps an hour or so. When asked whether she and her companion, Alice B. Toklas, who spent the war years in the countryside outside Paris, ever gave up hope about the future, she replied, "No, we knew the Americans would come and liberate us." That got a bad review from the GIs present who did not like their liberation efforts taken for granted or the assumption that we would automatically come to France's rescue. But it was a splendid experience

© 1945 The Plain Dealer. All rights reserved. Reprinted with permission.

to see the famous expatriate author who focused her comments on the dignity of the common man.

When V-E Day finally arrived on 8 May 1945 it was both a relief and an anti-climax since it had been widely predicted for some time. First, we had to celebrate at a raucous party that I planned at an Antwerp bar which quickly got out of control, but no one cared. Everyone was overjoyed thanks to the powerful

Beer and champagne made these 105th guys happy at the Magic Palace bar in Antwerp. So did the fact that they were celebrating V-E Day, 9 May 1945.

combination of a great victory plus beer, champagne and cognac. The noise from the delirious crowd and the band was at a high sustained level. The Belgique girls looked prettier than ever and entered into the festivities with equal fervor. And as the song goes "we could have danced all night." The pictures taken at that event show a rowdy but totally happy group.

Even happier were the people of Antwerp as I wrote in a letter:

You can't imagine how happy they were. They went wild! It was impossible not to absorb some of their spirit... They sang, danced and paraded in the streets even the day after V-E Day...the trams did not run for three days... There were mobs of joyous people...flags everywhere...rockets and ack-ack tracers lit up the sky...I'll long remember the sight of those Belgian people, so happy because the bloodshed...the V-1s and V-2s...were over.[52]

Then we had to wonder what comes next; with low point scores we knew we weren't going home very soon. The army had set up a point system to permit an orderly, prioritized method

The so-called "little red schoolhouse" in Reims where the German surrender was signed ending the war in Europe.

for getting all the troops home. Points were awarded for months in the army, months overseas, battle stars, Purple Hearts, children, etc. and those with the highest point totals went home first, an arrangement so logical and fair that it must have been invented by somebody other than the army.

With the European war over our work schedule eased and we had some opportunities for fun. In late June, thirty of us jumped at the chance to truck down to Namur, Belgium, for a party sponsored by the women from the Women's Army Corps (WAC) at the Chat-Noir (Black Cat) country club. When we arrived at the club, thanks to a typical army foul-up, the party was being held somewhere else in Namur. Most of the guys opted to stay at the club to swim, relax, drink and goof off or go to the nearby Red Cross. Paul Grady and I were the only ones who kept our priorities straight and we took off (like hound dogs in heat) to find the party and the girls — cherchez la femmes — which we did. My reaction was that it "was grand to see and hear some American girls again...the party seemed a bit of America transported to Belgium...but the beverage was an odd concoction of GI grapefruit juice and cognac. Darn good though"!

Before we departed from Antwerp each of us were awarded impressive certificates that read:

The People of the City of Antwerp:

This certificate is awarded in appreciation of, and as a token of, gratitude for work in the Port of Antwerp during the one hundred and seventy five days of continuous enemy air and V-weapons attacks between October 7, 1944 and March 30, 1945.

Antwerp

On behalf of the Board of Burgomaster and Aldermen.

THE PEOPLE OF

The City of Antwerp

To all to whom these presents shall come, greetings.
This certificate is awarded to

Cpl. George N. Havens,
105th Port Marine Maint. Co.

in appreciation of, and as a token of gratitude
for his work in the Port of Antwerp during the
one hundred seventy five days of continuous enemy
air and V.-weapon attacks between October 7,
1944 and March 30, 1945.

Antwerp, 4 th. September 1945.

ON BEHALF OF THE BOARD OF BURGOMASTER AND ALDERMEN:

By Order:
The Town Clerk,

The Burgomaster,

Certificate presented to all members of the 105th for their
service in Antwerp during the aerial and V-weapon attacks of
1944-45.

So we had shared the vicious Nazi V-bomb assault with the brave Belgians. We had survived, the city had survived and the port had achieved its mission but the cost was 3,752 civilians killed, 6000 injured, and 731 Allied military personnel killed, 1192 injured.

. . .

The Stars and Stripes 8 May 1945

CHAPTER TWENTY

We're Done in Europe. On to the Pacific.

Once again we were confronted the uncertainty of the army as we waited and guessed about our future. The obvious options were to continue our mission in Antwerp, serve as part of the close-out force in the ETO, join the army of occupation in Germany, or move on to the Pacific where the war against Japan was entering its climactic phase.

We got our answer to our future quickly: we were going direct to the Pacific — not via the U.S. — to help defeat the Japanese. The prospect of a 30-to-40 day trip on a crowded, steamy hot, troop ship through the Mediterranean Sea, Suez Canal, Red Sea, Indian Ocean, and China Sea into the Pacific Ocean filled us with a certain dread. Even worse it would be taking us to the other side of the world and even farther from home.

Once again we used humor to lighten up an unhappy situation as we speculated when we might actually get home. Would it be "Home alive in '45" or "Out of the sticks in '46" or "From hell to heaven in '47" or the popular favorite "Golden Gate in '48."

But first on 7 July we once again boarded "40&8" cars and moved to an Assembly Area Camp (AAC) which had been set up on the Champagne Plain near Mailly de Camp to process those units who were headed to the Pacific Theater. There were a series of such redeployment camps, all named for well-known American cities. How thoughtful of the army to remind us of home when we couldn't go there. After a slow 36-hour trip we ended up in Camp New Orleans, an amazing coincidence since New Orleans was where the 105th originated.

My letter home characterized the trip:

All the way everybody waves at us and we wave back. Men, women, children, everybody waves — so many that you'd think we were a special train. All the kids run out near the tracks — just multitudes of them — and all the fellows throw them gum and candy. They really go for it. Down in southern Belgium t h e people were very friendly. When the train would stop they would come out to talk and give us fruit. We give them highly-prized American cigarettes in return. There was real friendship...in spite

Launcelot and Alice Havens reading one of their son's 300 wartime letters which they preserved and the author used to write this book.

of language, cultural and national differences. The civilians grateful to the GIs for their liberation and the GIs amply repaid to see the happy children and smiling parents.[53]

At the entrance to Camp New Orleans some sadistic individual had erected a large overhead sign in Oriental letters that proclaimed "On to Tokyo." Its inspiration was lost on most of us. Our company accommodations were basic: a series of 6-man

Our tent city at Camp New Orleans on the Champagne Plain, France, where we spent 108 days waiting to go to the Pacific Theater. "Doc" Albro in background.

pyramidal tents, a quonset hut for a mess hall and plenty of open space. The camp itself had a Red Cross building, a big open-air theater (later replaced by a huge airplane hangar enclosure), other facilities and lots of German POWs, who did all of the scut work like kitchen KP and menial work around the camp. All we had to do for 108 days was to stand one formation in the morning, then we were on our own. It was hot, it was dry, not raining at one

The headquarters team of the 105th: (L to R) Louis Good, Duane "Doc" Albro, Wayne Ankrum and Ray Buehler.

point for 30 straight days, it was boring. We had to devise our own techniques for maintaining our morale, which was dented by the return of the censorship of our mail. Apparently it would have been a major breach of army secrecy to let the Japanese know that the vaunted 105th was coming to the Pacific Theater. Did they really think that my parents were communicating regularly with Tojo and Hirohito?

Fortunately, we had Early D. Langford from Tennessee who had played on his state championship volleyball team, so he introduced us to volleyball. We built a court, liberated a net, posts and a ball, and started learning the game from Early. We played almost every day and acquired reasonable skill, though most of us could not learn how to dive halfway across the court to dig out a shot as Early often did.

In the evenings we had our 105th Hill Billy Band to entertain us and this was true Americana. Think about these names of the players. On fiddle (which was played off the hip) was our First Sergeant Holmes G. Law from West Virginia (he had quickly earned the nickname of Holmes G. "I am the F—ing" Law). On

First Sergeant Holmes G. Law of West Virginia exhibited a tough manner but always took good care of his men and played a mean fiddle.

Camp New Orleans was hot, dry and boring for the author but volleyball, our 105th "Hill Billy" Band, and trips to Paris helped.

banjo was Jewel Parker from Texas who could really pick tunes like "Under the Double Eagle." On guitar was our multi-talented Early D. Langford from Tennessee. And on mandolin from Hopewell, Virginia, was Louis Grover Good. When they got going on those familiar country and blue grass numbers, they were something special.

The well-organized USO did provide first-rate entertainment for us as we were treated to Jane Froman, the Shep Fields and Hal McIntyre Bands, Celeste Holm, and the Radio City Music Hall revue with the Rockettes. At some shows there were some 5,000 GIs all sitting on the ground, responding loudly and yearning for home.

I continued a practice started in England of reading as many books as possible on philosophy, with most books sent to me by my folks. I read Will Durant's books and those by Aristotle, Plato, William James, Spinoza, Kant, Hegel, Schopenhauer, Voltaire, Locke and many others, all of which I still have in my library. It filled the hours and it satisfied an intellectual craving amidst the non-intellectual army existence.

The food was rotten. It was the common belief that the mess officer and the mess sergeant were apparently selling some of our good rations on the black market and giving us the rest. On many occasions we simply went through the mess line, as required, picked up the slop, walked right through the mess hall, dumped our uneaten food, washed our mess kits, threw them in our tents and proceeded to the Red Cross for coffee and doughnuts. I have often remarked that the Red Cross kept us alive, an exaggeration with much truth.

At Camp New Orleans I was not too far from Mourmelonle-Petit where Bud Ketchum was based. We exchanged several home-and-home visits which were great fun. The most notable was a Sunday jeep excursion from Bud's camp with Charlie Gardiner (a Case Sigma Nu), Ed Kowsz, Bud and myself. We headed north with Liège as our goal passing through Vouziers and Charleville in France and then along the Meuse River to Givet, Fumay, Dinant, and Namur in Belgium. In one scary incident, we were racing along when we saw people waving at us frantically. We learned their purpose as we screeched to a halt before a

The author with Morgan "Bud" Ketchum at his company area at Mourmelon-le-Petit, France, on one of the frequent occasions we met during the army years.

frail barrier blocking a bombed out bridge. The irony was that the bridge had been destroyed in World War I! We never did reach Liege but it was a memorable, fun trip up one side of the Meuse, back on the other side, 300 miles in all.

• • • •

Whenever possible we cadged one-day passes to go to Paris. Adding the times I had been there from Antwerp, the I&E School, and a three-day pass, I visited Gay Paree perhaps 6 or 8 times. I do recall that I spent three complete Sunday afternoons in the Louvre Museum viewing Venus de Milo, Winged Victory, the great works of art and, of course, the Mona Lisa. As we viewed Da Vinci's masterpiece the little old French guard made a profound comment in his broken English: "Remember, you are not judging; you are being judged by the painting." For someone naive about great art, it was an insight into the French perspective on art and its unique position in their culture.

The gathering place to meet other GIs in Paris was the Rainbow Corners Red Cross located near the Place de l'Opera. In these visits I did all the usual tourist spots and was always filled with awe, Paris being the one city where the reality exceeded my expectations. It was especially rewarding to stand on the Trocadero balcony, where the famous photo of a conquering and joyous Adolf Hitler had been taken as he viewed the Eiffel Tower, and know that we had beaten the Nazis.

On one occasion in Paris, Paul Grady, Duane Albro and I encountered Captain Doran who graciously invited us to dine with him at the Officers' Club, a real treat given the food at camp. Little did we realize at that time that Grady's last assignment in the ETO six months later would be as the non-com running an Officers' Club.

And so the hot, dry days at Camp New Orleans ran on until one day in August the rains came and on 6 August so did the

Two of the 105th's mavericks, Cyrus Dolbeare and Russ Casadonti, spoof Hitler and the Nazi salute to signify our victory in Europe.

news of a new, powerful bomb which had been dropped on Hiroshima. We ignored the rain and raced from tent to tent spreading the news and speculating on its impact on our future. Then on 9 August came the Nagasaki bomb, and shortly thereafter on 15 August the Japanese surrender. Suddenly it was over and the war that had started in 1939 had come to an abrupt end. None of us had anticipated anything remotely like this and we hardly knew how to react. But we knew that the planned invasion of the Japanese mainland with its horrendous casualties was no longer necessary. We knew that our Pacific trip had been canceled just in time. We later learned that our orders had us scheduled to ship direct to Manila in the Philippines. Somehow missing that trip did not cause any regrets.

As August stretched endlessly into September the waiting and uncertainty about our postwar destiny generated a liberal amount of understandable griping. Our officers knew nothing, we knew nothing but the word from various parents in the States was that some other Port Marine Maintenance Companies had arrived home. The ironical and infuriating situation was that of the six PMM units at Camp Gordon Johnston (105th, 106th, 107th, 108th, 109th and 110th), we were the first to ship overseas, we

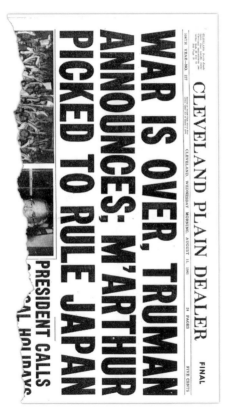

CLEVELAND PLAIN DEALER

104TH YEAR—NO. 227   CLEVELAND, WEDNESDAY MORNING, AUGUST 15, 1945   24 PAGES   FINAL   FIVE CENTS

WAR IS OVER, TRUMAN ANNOUNCES; M'ARTHUR PICKED TO RULE JAPAN

PRESIDENT CALLS

did the best work in the most important port and were the only unit in danger (from aerial and V-bomb bombardment). The other PMM units were at Rouen, Le Havre, Cherbourg, Marseille, and England, yet we were the only company still left overseas. Somehow the army thought we deserved this reward.

. . .

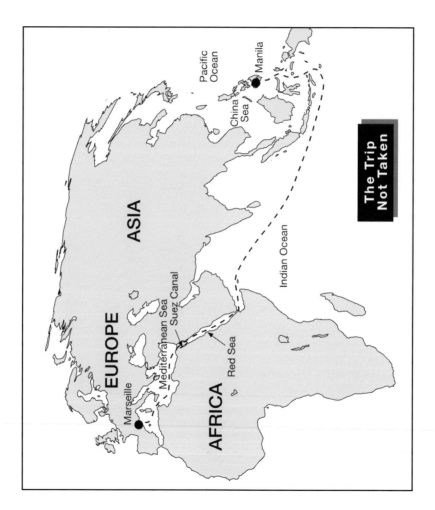

The Trip Not Taken: *After two atomic bombings Japan surrendered, avoiding an assault on its mainland and canceling the author's long Marseille-to-Manila sea voyage.*

CHAPTER TWENTY-ONE

The War is Over But We Can't Go Home

So we continued to play the army waiting game all over again. What was next for us? After enduring two more months of army uncertainty, on 23 October the 105th was disbanded and we learned that ten of us including Ray Buehler, Verne Niemi, Joe Hermann, Perry Richardson, Fred Stinnett, Ned Goldin and others — were assigned to the 3617th Heavy Duty Truck Company based in Champigny, a tiny village five kilometers from Reims. Headquarters was on an estate in a modest chateau with comfortable tents arrayed around the grounds for most of us.

We had a sizable contingent of German POWs who did all of the routine, menial work. They lived in smaller tents and fox holes dug into the ground, some rather elaborate and well protected against the snow and cold. A complement of Polish and Yugoslav guards watched the Germans. Admittedly, it was quite satisfying to see the soldiers of the "master race" being servile and compliant, and doing the dirty work for us.

About 400 yards away was the motor pool, dispatch office, and the repair garage manned by skilled German mechanics. The company had 48 semis — Whites, Autocars, Internationals, GMCs, Federals — and an equal number of

10-ton trailers. Our mission was to transport strategic material and supplies all over the ETO including Germany. The drivers vied to get assigned to the smooth-running, faster Internationals and GMCs which were the best semis, the others were slow and clunky.

It turned out that ours was the last *white, GI, heavy duty* truck company in the Channel Base Section (France, Belgium, Luxembourg, Netherlands). Since the army was segregated, there were *black* truck companies. Since we had won the war, there were German *POW* truck companies but we were a unique company in the segregated, postwar ETO close-out force. We handled shipments to Munich, Frankfort, Marseille, Stuttgart, and even Berlin. To reach Berlin our trucks had to go through the Russian Occupation Zone and things with the Reds were prickly and somewhat hostile. We armed our drivers with sidearms and told them to ignore any Russian checkpoints, keep going and head on into the American Zone in Berlin. Fortunately we had no ugly incidents.

In one of our most critical and strategic assignments, we transported a 10-ton trailer full of condoms and prophylactic kits to Berlin. I'm not sure what the GIs there were doing, but clearly the U.S. Army's "No Fraternization" policy had gone to hell.

In a sad moment in December 1945 we dispatched three trucks, washed and parade-ground shiny, to the American Military Cemetery at Hamm, Luxembourg for the funeral of General George S. Patton Jr., acknowledged by the Germans as the Allies best battlefield commander.

Before long I was promoted to be the chief dispatcher with the rank of sergeant. It had been a long 18 months from the time in New Orleans when I had made corporal, a period of some frustration at being repeatedly passed over. In the early New Orleans days of the 105th, I had been promoted to corporal and acted as a platoon leader until we entered the technical training and technical work phase of our mission. Then I was bypassed as our skilled mechanical and technical people got the stripes and I remained a lowly corporal. To be fair, I did not have the work experience they did and only a partial college education, but the deciding factor was undoubtedly my involvement in the Falmouth demonstration which was seen as a de facto "mutiny."

Now I was in charge of dispatching our trucks and drivers on their daily assignments, scheduling maintenance for our trucks and trailers, overseeing the repair garage, and completing and filing lengthy reports with our higher authority in Reims. Within less than a month I got two more promotions, so after three years since enlisting I was now a Tech Sergeant with five lovely stripes on my arm. But best of all I had a splendid partner to work with in the dispatch office, John Perry Richardson of

John Perry Richardson and the author made a great team as they ran the dispatch operations for the 3617th Heavy Duty Truck Co. in Champigny, France.

Northwood Center, New Hampshire. Perry had been drafted out of the Portsmouth Navy Yard and had joined the 105th late in its life. He was a fine human being, easy to work with, highly capable and with a droll sense of humor. He would frequently display his New England accent by proclaiming that "I'm going to get in my cah and go get a Hershey bah." Our family visited Perry, his wife Evelyn and daughter in New Hampshire on one of our postwar camping trips.

Perry and I had it made. We lived in a large pyramidal tent, our "canvas chateau," next to the dispatch tent, just the two of us, with good beds. It was equipped with a stove so we were warm and cozy all through the tough French winter, and could brew up coffee and heat up snacks as needed. And we had a jeep at our disposal, primarily to take reports into Reims, but for personal use, too.

Each of our 48 semis was assigned to a specific driver and was identified by a six-digit number. After a little practice I could call up the six-digit number of each driver's vehicle from memory as I made up the dispatch ticket. This never failed to

John Perry Richardson displays his million-dollar smile in front of one of the 48 tractor-trailer rigs we used to help close out operations in the ETO.

astound the drivers. I would simply look up to see who the driver was, then write down his vehicle number.

A mile or so down the winding, low-lying road toward Reims was the village center and town hall of Champigny. We commandeered the unheated hall on some nights to show American movies where the audience was strictly segregated — GIs seated up front, local French folks next, and German POWs in the rear, usually standing, and French kids everywhere. We also used the village *hotel de ville* for our parties which were wild and unsupervised. Our guys would buy good French champagne for a few bucks but then treat it like beer, swilling it down in great gulps. The results were predictable, not pretty and even dangerous since after the party we had to drive trucks and jeeps back to our quarters along a narrow road that almost always had an impenetrable fog. In some cases, the front seat passenger would lean out of the vehicle with a flashlight to locate the edge of the roadway so as to guide the driver.

Our stay in Champigny was some six months and in midwinter our likable company captain was severely injured in a jeep accident. As he traveled in a blinding snowstorm on the highway to Soissons he suddenly saw two French bicyclists in his path, swerved the jeep and hit one of the handsome trees that line many French highways head-on. A passing French pick-up truck got him into the back of the truck, threw a tarp over him and brought him to our area. We immediately wrapped him in blankets, carefully moved him into one of our trucks and took him to the army hospital in Reims. He survived but we never saw him again as he was transferred to England or the States.

Concurrent with the arrival of our new Commanding Officer, our first sergeant was redeployed back to the States. In a surprising move, the C.O. promoted me to first sergeant to "run the company" — after all, it was a truism that the sergeants ran the army. It was a proud moment for me as I sewed on the six stripes-and-diamond insignia of a "top sergeant." I took over operations in the HQ office and Perry ran the dispatch operation. To help me I had a two German POW clerk-typists, one named George Junk whose home was in Hanover in the German Russian zone. He had worked in New York as an architect, spoke excellent English and was quite efficient. He could even discern mistakes in English that GIs would make when they came into the HQ.

On 6 March 1946 the C.O. put me in for an Army Commendation Ribbon citing my leadership of the truck company as reflected in its highly efficient and effective operations.

• • • •

Reims: The Cathedral, Champagne and Camille

There were three memorable non-military attractions in Reims. It was a profound experience to see the great Reims Cathedral, considered one of the finest Gothic cathedrals in Europe. It had been badly damaged in World War I and then restored with funds from John D. Rockefeller (who started The Standard Oil Co. in Cleveland and had his Forest Hill summer estate and mansion near my home in East Cleveland). Fortunately it emerged relatively unscathed from WWII. Nearby is the golden statue of Jeanne d'Arc at the site where she brought the Dauphine in 1429 to be crowned. Now over 500 years later I was at that historic spot, reflecting that we had helped liberate France so it could now have the chance to recover its glory, badly tarnished by the 1940 collapse, the Nazi occupation and the Vichy collaboration.

And, of course, Reims boasts the great Champagne caves of Mumm's, Pommery, Greno, Piper Heidsieck and other famous brands. And, of course, we quickly developed a taste for only the best champagne as we continually celebrated our victory. The surrender documents for that victory had been signed by the Germans in the nearby so-called "little red schoolhouse" in Reims, which somehow was not red nor little. Somehow I never got around to visiting the champagne caves, a grievous oversight.

The third attraction was Camille, a French jeune fille. Champigny was not much of a village but there was a brick factory there, adjacent to our motor pool. I soon became acquainted with the teen-age daughter of one of the workmen at the factory, Camille Michon, one of eight children in the Michon family. Her father was the only male member of his greater family still alive, his father, brothers, cousins and others had all been killed in WWI or WWII, a tragic statement about the impact of the wars on France.

In one of my letters home I described her situation:

She is only 17, but quite mature and attractive. I guess I got acquainted with her at one of our company dances. Also I've seen her at other dances, have driven her home in the jeep after the company movie and so forth. I took her to the Couples Club in Reims where I met up with Paul Grady.

For some time now I've taken my candy ration over to her house for her four brothers and three sisters — all younger than she. The family of ten lives in a small house, in America it would be called a shack.

They've shown me their weekly food rations — and well you just wouldn't believe it. I don't see how they can get along on it...yet you have to admire their uncomplaining attitude. So I've taken over coffee, oranges, candy, soap...and a case of army "10-in-1" rations.

She has a wonderful sense of humor and I like to see her laugh. Wednesday night I talked with the whole family and then took her for a ride in the jeep. Friday night I took her to the French movie in Reims.[54]

With my fractured French and her basic English, Camille and I somehow communicated and became friends. I invited her to our company movies several times in the unheated village hall. Despite the cold she wore only a man's suit jacket, probably her

Camille Michon was a special friend during the Champigny days. Her father was the only male left in his extended family after the carnage of two world wars.

Camille attended the French ecole in Reims which required a five kilometer (3 mile) walk each way. Since I had to deliver my reports to HQ in Reims each morning I frequently gave Camille and her girl friends a ride to town in my jeep. For her own reasons, she invariably insisted that I drop them off several blocks from the school, rather than drive them right up to the door.

As spring started to arrive in Champigny, Camille invited me to have two dinners with her family in their extremely mod-

father's, but never complained about the cold and refused all offers of army clothing. She also attended our company parties along with other French young ladies.

est home on my last Saturday and Sunday there. The first meal the entire family shared one chicken which was small, chewy, tough and probably quite old. Everyone, even the children had red wine, and to make it go further each diluted their wine with water. On Sunday I brought them three one-gallon cans of pears and peaches, that I had liberated from our kitchen storeroom and a bottle of Creme de Menthe. You would have thought I had brought them gold. That day we had one roast rabbit which I ate for the first time in my life along with red wine, bread, potatoes and cheese. Despite their meager situation they displayed warm generosity in sharing what they had with me.

After that second dinner Camille and I took a long walk in the warm March afternoon sunshine and I revealed to her that I would shortly be going back to Etats Unis. In an unforgettable, touching moment she then sang "Gonna Take a Sentimental Journey" to me in French. Wartime infatuations have a poignant quality conjured up by the foreign setting, lonesomeness, and the haunting need for feminine companionship and tenderness. Most do not last, or if they do, end up badly. But they add momentary joy to one's life. Even more, Camille taught me to understand and like the French people.

Just before I did depart she gave me her picture with an inscription on the back. I expected it to be some expression of affection or love, but it simply said "To a friend from a young French girl for our liberation...Camille." Well, as we learned to say, c'est le guerre.

• • •

The author finally earned his first sergeant stripes and learned that the sergeants really do run the army.

CHAPTER TWENTY-THREE

What the Army Teaches

The Talmud proclaims that "Learning is achieved only in company." That may be one reason that the army was a profound learning experience for me as I think it was for many. The army was a testing ground and a real-world classroom that taught me many things including:

- That the world is big, diverse, difficult, and sometimes dangerous.
- To retain and practice the basic values I had been taught.
- To assume responsibility for myself and my behavior.
- To provide enlightened leadership for others I might command.
- To broaden my perspectives of other people, their beliefs, and their lifestyles.
- Appreciation of the richness and diversity of other countries and their cultures.
- Many basic skills and survival practices useful throughout life but especially in camping, hiking and backpacking.
- That the loving support of family, friends and a sweetheart is beyond value.

This learning experience has led me to the conviction that national service for all young people would be beneficial to them as well as their country and our world. We know that freedom is not free and requires the efforts and sacrifices of many people if it is to survive. Given that we proclaim that all people are created equal and are equal before the law, should not their obligation to contribute to their nation and their society also be equal.

Recall the inspired words of John F. Kennedy, "Ask not what your country can do for you. Ask what you can do for your country." Recall the great contribution that the Civilian Conservation Corps of the New Deal era made to our parks, forests and natural resources during the nine years that it provided work and training for 500,000 men. Recall the global impact and good will that the Peace Corps has generated over the last 40 years.

Now think about the multiple benefits that would accrue from the service of all young people for a year or two as they participated in their choice of the military, Peace Corps, Americorps, or other organizations devoted to educational, health care, conservation or similar pursuits. Think of the positive consequences for our quality of life, our standard of living, our national pride, and the personal growth of these individuals.

America has long been a world leader in the extent of its volunteerism in religious, charitable, civic and cultural activities, so this would be a logical extension of that practice.

No one group or class should be induced or expected to make an unfair or unequal contribution or sacrifice. All citizens should earn the rights and privileges of living in the United States through national service.

• • • • •

I also learned that among the many skills needed to survive in the army, two are critically important — the ability to kill time and the ability to improvise and cobble up things to improve one's situation.

There is a lot of "hurry up and wait" activity and/or just plain waiting. I guess it's inevitable in an organization the size, complexity and newness of the wartime U.S. Army. So you wait for everything. You wait in the mess line. You wait in the latrine line. You wait to get inspected, injected, and instructed. You wait to get your mail, your pay, and your equipment. You wait for your next assignment, your next promotion, and your next KP detail. You wait — usually in the rain or the hot sun — while your officers confer endlessly about what to do next. You wait to go overseas and then you wait to go home. Waiting can be deadly and boring unless you learn how to be a killer, a killer of time. You can't endure the army unless you know how to wait creatively and effectively...

While you're waiting, it's a good time to think up ingenious ways to make your daily existence at least tolerable. During the 100-degree days of Camp Wheeler we initiated our learning by pouring baking soda on our prickly heat rashes, talc into our sweaty socks, and salt tablets into our aching guts. In our Falmouth, England hotel we jiggered up a gas line for our fireplace to keep our room warm, built a volley ball court, ate local fish and chips instead of army chow, fixed up the hotel gardens, and added a radio PA system for our quarters.

In the muddy field near LeHavre, France we found shelter from the incessant rain in a deserted hut, slept in a farmer's hayloft, and slipped off to a nearby facility for our weekly shower. On the "40 & 8" train to Antwerp we scrounged apples from local trees and calvados from nearby farmhouses whenever we stopped. Even better, in our cold boxcar we rigged up a stove out of some tin cans and used some gasoline we swiped at one stop, so we could heat up coffee and some cans of stew.

In Antwerp's Luchtbal barracks we upgraded a bare, Spartan facility with shelves, coat racks, library, radios, pin-up pictures, and other amenities.

And in the Champigny truck company Richardson and I achieved total creature comfort — a heated, weatherized pyramidal tent with a door, an inside lowered ceiling to maximize the warmth, hospital beds instead of cots, radio, telephone, coat racks, cupboard, and stocks of food and beverages.

The key is to see this exercise as a challenge to your ingenuity, your creativity, your individuality, your ability to "moonlight requisition" what you needed — and most of all to make your life seem less like the army.

. . . .

The army also provided my first lessons in how to negotiate effectively. Each of us could buy a carton of cigarettes periodically at the Post Exchange, but as a non-smoker I simply sold them on the black market to earn some extra funds to supplement my meager pay. When I encountered the little Belgian black marketeer behind a building, I would always ask, "How much will you give me for a carton of American cigarettes"? He would invariably shake his head and respond in broken English, "No, you speak first." If I named a high figure he would groan, moan and refuse to deal, but if my figure was low, the deal was done immediately. It became clear to me that the one who "speaks first" in any negotiation is usually at a disadvantage, an insight that served me well in later years.

. . . .

They say the army builds men. It's true. I entered the army at 156 pounds and arrived home weighing 172 with a bulk that almost terminated Ginnie's affection for me. But there was a logical, unavoidable explanation: once again it was army food. A memorable meal that we were served in Champigny defines the problem — it featured macaroni and cheese, mashed potatoes and gravy, creamed corn, bread and butter, and for dessert, bread pudding. That's starch and carbos done the army way.

. . . .

CHAPTER TWENTY-FOUR

The Long Voyage Home

From the truck company in Champigny I was sent in a German 3rd Class Compartment railroad car with wooden seats to a "cigarette camp" for redeployment back to the U.S. Once again there was a string of these camps on the French coast named after the leading cigarette brands such as Lucky Strike or Chesterfield, a telling commentary on the promotional power of the tobacco companies. I ended up at Camp Herbert Tareyton near Le Havre POE assigned to the 482nd Engineer Maintenance Co. with 267 enlisted men and 7 officers. In the army's wisdom, someone had to take all the units in the ETO and their records home to the States. We would be the carrier for the 482nd and the 482nd would carry us home.

Within the first hour I was summoned to the captain's HQ where I joined two master sergeants, a battalion sergeant major and another first sergeant, a grand gathering of five six-stripers. The captain explained that he had gotten instructions from the camp commander which required that we get everyone's individual records —personnel, medical, clothing, equipment—and the company records in order and up to date before we could even get on a waiting list for a ship. Then he dropped a small bombshell, "Havens, you're to be the first sergeant in charge of this unit to get us home." I protested that I was the youngest six striper there and had the shortest time in grade, that others were certainly more qualified. He was adamant, I was the one. I looked around at the other guys and said, "OK, but I sure need lots of help from all of you."

Quickly I called the entire complement of the 482nd together and explained the drill — everything had to be in order before we could even get in line. I asked a rhetorical question, "Who wants to go home"? This produced a roar of positive response. Then I issued a challenge, "Let's set a new camp record. Let's get our work done faster than any unit in this camp ever has so we can get back home." It had the desired effect as we mobilized for action, started from scratch, worked all that day, that night until 3 am, and all the next day to complete the requirements. The experienced battalion sergeant major took on the complicated personnel records task, grabbed some volunteers, and updated the records of all the men. A staff sergeant named Rosenberg from Brooklyn supervised the clothing problems, getting everyone their full, proper clothing issue. Others handled various tasks with speed and high spirits. It was a happy madhouse but then we were ready to get in line for a ship.

I left Europe from the same place I had arrived — Le Havre — this time on the *Sea Devil*, a C-4 merchant ship, the type that had been mass produced in U.S. shipbuilding yards. The knock on these ships was that they had been produced in two halves, then welded together, but in some cases the ships had come apart at the weld and sunk. Since our ship had seen service in both the Atlantic and Pacific Oceans, the subject of metal fatigue was a constant concern as we headed toward home. Adding to the anxiety was the fact that stormy weather in the North Atlantic forced us to detour well to the south, but we still hit rough seas. One rogue wave caused to ship to roll as much as it had in an earlier typhoon off Okinawa, one of the ship's company informed us.

Our comfy, cozy quarters were in the front hold of the

ship which had been converted into an high-capacity bunkroom with pipe rail bunks extending six high. As we lay in our bunks we could see the front steel hull plates deflecting and bending as the ship plowed through the high waves. Perhaps this was an army test for claustrophobia or paranoia before they were to discharge us. This was only my second ocean cruise, but after this experience I would not take another one for 55 years.

While the voyage took us ten days due to the southerly route, I remember little about it. Each day seemed just like the previous one with vast expanses of water. After all there aren't many recognizable landmarks in mid-ocean. What I do remember with great clarity is our dramatic early evening entrance into New York harbor just as it was getting dark. As we glided by the lighted Statue of Liberty, everyone on board rushed to that side of the ship. Luckily we did not capsize right there within sight of our goal.

Seeing the Statue of Liberty was an incredible and powerful experience for all of us. She was the symbol of all we had fought for, but for three years we never knew whether we would see her again or not. As we passed "her" there was total silence on the ship; it was so quiet that you could have heard a tear drop. And many did. Somehow we now realized that we were home, that it was over, that we would be OK, that the United States of America was still there and victorious despite the brutal horrors unleashed by the Nazis and the Japanese. Most of us were speechless and profoundly grateful that we had made it because many of our comrades did not.

We docked somewhere on Manhattan Island and were immediately transferred to a ferry that would take us to the Jersey side for transfer to Camp Kilmer. During that ferry trip I had a marvelous experience as perhaps six guys in my unit came up to me and thanked me for getting them home. One of them even quipped that this was the first time he had ever seen a first sergeant do any real work. Given my 21 years of age and the heavy responsibility I had felt, I found it highly gratifying.

At Camp Kilmer we were processed once again. If the army is expert at one thing it is processing its personnel. A key part of the processing which we had already experienced at Camp Herbert Tareyton was a pitch to "re-up" and stay in the army. After all they emphasized, you've already got three years under your belt and in just 17 more years you could retire at half pay, or at 30 years get a full-pay pension. Somehow it was easy to decline this generous offer. The military is the largest alternative lifestyle in the U.S. but my experience offered no incentive to prolong my army service. Then it was time to say goodbye to guys we had gotten to know only two weeks ago as we were dispersed across the country for discharge.

My final army post was Camp Atterbury in Indiana where the main activity was more processing and more waiting before they handed me that wonderful Honorable Discharge from the U.S. Army on 8 April 1946. After three years and 127 days my combined reserve and active duty was over. On my Eisenhower jacket were three overseas hash marks for my 19 months in the ETO, a service stripe for my three years of active duty in the army, my first sergeant insignia, and ribbons for Good Conduct, American Theater, European Theater with one battle star, and the Victory medal. Not much compared to the "fruit salad" you see on generals or admirals, but I was proud of them. I had done my part.

I grabbed the first train for Cleveland, arrived in the early morning at the Terminal Tower, took a cab to 1889 Wymore Avenue, and rang the doorbell just as the folks were getting up. It hardly seemed real, but I was back home and it was glorious. My folks were overjoyed and anxious to hear more and more about my travels and experiences. And thankfully the family was back together again.

I changed from my army uniform into my regular clothes and started the next phase of my life as a civilian. The re-entry process took time as I slowly readjusted from

The author's high school sweetheart, the girl he came home to and married in 1948 while he was still in college.

the rigid regimentation of army life to the fun and freedom of being a discharged veteran. It was easy to adjust to my Mother's cooking which was always first-rate, to sleeping late, to reconnecting with friends, and to getting back on track with Ginnie.

• • • •

WE MADE THE HEADLINES POSSIBLE

CHAPTER TWENTY-FIVE

The Most Significant Event in My Life

I have come to understand that the World War II army experience had been the most significant event of my life. It was totally unexpected. It ripped me out of a comfortable civilian life and thrust me into the rigors, discipline and strangeness of military life and the dangers of a world war. It put me among complete strangers (except for Umstead and Ketchum) with whom I would live, train, and serve for three years. It moved me around the U.S. and then took me to Europe where I had the opportunity to see Cornwall, London, Brussels, Antwerp, and Paris, live among the British, Belgian and French people, and experience their customs, food, drink and lifestyles. It taught me the value of teamwork and the warm support of trusted comrades. Most of all it enabled me to realize how fortunate I was to have my parents, Virginia, friends, and my home. And how extraordinarily lucky I had been to return home in one piece with no injuries or wounds.

Making this army experience especially rewarding were the close friendships that evolved during the three years:

- At Camp Wheeler it was George Umstead and Bud Ketchum who made infantry basic training tolerable if not fun. They have continued as lifelong friends.

- At West Virginia University I developed a close relationship with Alexander "Georg" Georgalakis that continued during our time in New Orleans as he orchestrated many happy and fun times for us. We had many similar likes and dislikes, and respected each other's intelligence.

- In New Orleans the strong camaraderie of the ASTPers — Duane "Doc" Albro, Ray Buehler, Louis Good, Paul Grady, Roy McKernan — emerged and endured through the rest of the 105th days and its recent reunions.

- At that time Paul Grady became a valued friend and buddy. Paul was in the terms of that day a "hot sketch" and a "holy terror." He seemed the luckiest guy I'd ever known as he was always in the right place at the right time. He saw Churchill, Eisenhower and other leaders. But the ultimate was that he was in Paris on V-E Day with the captain's jeep and *without* the captain! He

The captain's jeep driver; the irrepressible Paul Grady, who had a unique chance to celebrate V-E Day in Paris.

resurfaced at the company three days later. His final assignment in Europe was as the non-com running an Officers Club in Paris with outstanding entrepreneurial opportunities to enhance his Swiss bank account. Paul and I shared many times and experiences together, including visiting with him in Paris and two visits in Reims and Champigny (later I would connect up with him in 1950 in Swampscott, Massachusetts and he would visit our first Cleveland home in the mid-50s).

- In the 3617 Truck Company I truly enjoyed working and living with the affable John Perry Richardson in the dispatch office. No one could have had a finer partner than I did.

  Enduring the stress, boredom, loneliness, frustration, uncertainty and danger of my military experience without the support, encouragement, humor and mutual concern of these fine individuals would have made it very different, very tough. Their friendship was invaluable and indispensable.

  Even though that was long ago the memories of those men and many others, our exploits and our escapades, and our time together burn brightly. It had been, indeed, an unforgettable experience. We had helped make the headlines possible. And the headlines proclaimed a wonderful victory over the Axis powers and their threat to our civilization. Working together as an unbeatable team, the front-line soldiers and the rear echelon troops had achieved their mission and secured the peace.

• • • •

The Cleveland Press

The Newspaper That Serves Its Readers

VICTORY EDITION

CLEVELAND, WEDNESDAY, AUGUST 15, 1945

NO. 27,285 — 5 Cents

PEACE

© 1945 *The Cleveland Press*

Chronology of
My World War II Experiences

7 December 1941 — Japanese bomb Pearl Harbor.

8 December 1941 — U.S. declares war on Japan.

11 December 1941 — Germany and Italy declare war on the U.S. which declares war on them.

1 December 1942 — Enlisted in the Army's Enlisted Reserve Corps. (ERC) Assigned Army Service Number: 15358862.

22 May 1943 — Called to active duty, sent to Camp Perry, Ohio.

3 June 1943 — Arrival at Camp Wheeler, Georgia, an Infantry Replacement Training Center, for basic training.

September 1943 — Completed 13 weeks of basic training, assigned to ASTP unit at West Virginia University, Morgantown, West Virginia.

April-May 1944	Completed two quarters of ASTP education. ASTP disbanded. Sent to "repple depple" at Camp Plauche, New Orleans, then assigned to the newly formed 105th Port Marine Maintenance Co.
16 May 1944	Transferred to New Orleans Army Air Base. Underwent unit training, earned Senior Life Saving badge.
5 June 1944	Promoted to corporal (T/5 rank).
6 June 1944	D-Day invasion of Normandy
1-2 July 1944	105th transferred to Camp Gordon Johnston, Florida for final training.
20-22 August 1944	Moved by train to Camp Miles Standish, Taunton, Massachusetts, with Boston as our Port of Embarkation.
29 August 1944	Boarded U.S. Mariposa troopship for movement to European Theater of Operations.
30 August 1944	Departed from Boston Harbor.
7 September 1944	Arrival in Liverpool, England, then movement by train to Falmouth, Cornwall, for duties at U.S. Navy Repair Base.

13 November 1944	Movement by train to Southampton and by ship to Le Havre, encampment in the "muddy field" near Agincourt for a week.
21-24 November 1944	Movement by "40 & 8" cars to Antwerp, Belgium, quartered in Luchtbal Barracks.
28 November 1944	Arrival of first supply ship at Antwerp.
16 December 1944	Start of German Ardennes offensive, the Battle of the Bulge.
19 February 1945	German V-1 bomb hits Luchtbal Barracks killing 12 GIs in adjacent company.
March-April 1945	Attended I&E schools in Lille, France and Cite Universitaire, Paris.
30 March 1945	Last V-bomb incident in Antwerp.
7 May 1945	Germany surrenders unconditionally.
8 May 1945	V-E Day
7-9 July 1945	Movement to Camp New Orleans, Champagne Plain, France, one of the Assembly Area Camps for subsequent transfer to the Pacific Theater.

6 & 9 August 1945	Atom bombs dropped on Hiroshima and Nagasaki.
15 August 1945	Japan surrenders unconditionally.
2 September 1945	V-J Day and end of World War II.
23 October 1945	Assigned to the 3617th Heavy Duty Truck Co., Champigny, France. Served as dispatch sergeant.
28 December 1945	Promoted to Sergeant.
5 January 1946	Promoted to Staff Sergeant.
6 February 1946	Promoted to Tech Sergeant of the 3617th.
23 February 1946	Promoted to First Sergeant. Recommended for Army Commendation Ribbon.
18 March 1946	Transferred to Camp Herbert Tareyton near Le Havre POE as part of the 482nd Engineer Maintenance Co. Designated as First Sergeant of unit.
24 March 1946	Boarded C-4 merchant ship for redeployment to the U.S.
4 April 1946	Arrival in New York, moved to Camp Kilmer, New Jersey, then to Camp Atterbury, Indiana.

8 April 1946   Honorably discharged from the U.S. Army.

9 April 1946   Arrived home in East Cleveland, Ohio.

. . . .

Memorable Language from the Army Experience

Phrase	Explanation
Bird colonel	Full colonel; based on his insignia.
Blivet operation	An unhappy assignment expressed as "Ten pounds of crap in a five pound bag."
Blow it out your barracks bag!	Disagreement or disgust about anything.
Buck sergeant	Lowest rank of sergeant with three stripes.
"Buzz bomb" chicken	Meal served at Luchtbal Barracks.
Chicken shit routine	Activity that is mean, petty, and often unnecessary or useless.
Dismiss	The most welcome drill order.
Dog tags	Small brass I.D. tags worn on a chain around the neck which identify name, Army serial number, dates of tetanus-typhoid injections, blood type and religious preference.

ETO	European Theater of Operations.
Fall out aft of the fantail for mail call	Spoof announcement aboard ship
Fall out in raincoats and combat boots	Order for a "short arm" inspection for sexual disease.
Fall out with rifles and full field packs	Order prior to a march or other exercise.
Field strip those butts	Order to dispose of cigarettes by scattering remaining tobacco on the ground and rolling up the paper into a tiny ball.
FUBAR	Fouled Up Beyond All Recognition.
Full field inspection	Parade ground exercise where all equipment and field pack items are arranged in prescribed fashion on the ground for the colonel to inspect as he drives by in a jeep at 20 mph.
Gas !!	Order for a poison gas drill requiring immediate donning of a gas mask.
Go for a Section 8	Buck for discharge on mental grounds.
Hash marks	Uniform insignia indicating length of service.
Hup, two, three, four	March cadence.

Hurry up and wait — The army pace.

I.G. — Inspector General, an audit department.

Keep your eyes, ears and bowels open and your mouth shut — My father-in-law's advice as I entered the service — based on his WW I experience.

Kilroy was here — Sign that showed up everywhere.

KP — Kitchen police: peeling potatoes, scrubbing pans, etc.

Line up and dress right — Get into formation.

Lister bag — A large, canvas-bag water container suspended from a tripod, holding water purified by Hala-zone tablets, from which GIs filled their cups or canteens. Developed by Joseph Lister, English surgeon.

Maggie's drawers — Rifle range signal that the shot missed the target.

Moonlight requisitioning — Procuring items that are needed in an unofficial manner, usually at night.

NMI — Used when a GI had no middle name or initial as in James NMI Gordon

Police the area — all I want to see are assholes and elbows.

Order to clean up the grounds.

PX

Post Exchange, army convenience store.

Re-up

Re-enlist for another tour of duty.

Sad Sack

Cartoon character in Yank. A beaten-down, no-hope private eternally subjected to fatigue duty. Hence, any sorry, unskilled soldier.

SHAEF

Supreme Headquarters Allied Expeditionary Forces (Eisenhower's command).

Shit on a shingle

Creamed chipped beef on toast.

SNAFU

Situation Normal All Fouled Up.

Take ten

Welcome order for a ten minute break.

The flag is up. The flag is waving. Targets.

Sequence at the rifle range prior to firing.

There's the right way, the wrong way, and the Army way.

How things are done.

Three squares a day and a bed with my name on it, what more do I need.

Satisfaction with army life.

Top sergeant — First sergeant, highest non-com rank with six stripes and a diamond.

WAC — Women's Army Corps (earlier known as WAAC, Women's Auxiliary Army Corps)

We can't make you do anything, but we sure can make you wish you'd done it! — Warning to obey orders.

You'll be sorry — Warning about almost anything.

• • • •

Appendix A: Military Traffic at the Port of Antwerp
December 1944 to March 1946

Period	Deep draught ships		Stores coasters		M.T. Ships		Bulk edible oil ships		P.O.L. tankers	
	No. Ships	Tons	No. Ships	Tons	No. Ships	Tons	No. Ships	Tons	No. Ships	Tons
dec 44	49	259,332	22	18,666	67	9,932	1	1,480	21	16,693
jan 45	49	310,719	23	23,482	71	9,346	1	730	22	154,879
feb 45	43	263,906	30	29,373	65	7,406	0	0	17	129,650
mar 45	55	354,142	23	25,396	104	12,157	2	1,416	38	277,869
apr 45	60	379,645	42	56,365	73	8,686	3	8,590	41	288,800
may 45	74	461,861	35	35,465	37	6,122	3	3,971	33	254,898
jun 45	56	293,878	25	17,268	31	5,292	2	1,380	28	237,299
july 45	25	179,551	36	41,137	30	4,342	0	0	17	212,239
aug 45	27	180,737	60	80,307	31	5,144	2	8,914	23	237,103
sept 45	15	74,234	54	56,257	10	1,683	0	0	19	210,173
oct 45	10	61,138	22	26,215	11	715	0	0	18	187,723
nov 45	8	41,393	14	13,766	11	1,131	0	0	11	110,078
dec 45	4	11,903	13	13,828	8	872	0	0	5	18,881
jan 46	4	25,192	11	14,898	2	151	0	0	4	41,361
feb 46	2	15,067	10	10,620	9	532	0	0	5	58,005
mar 46	1	7,666	4	3,566	3	502	0	0	0	0

Note:

The Port of Antwerp opened to Allied military traffic on 28 November 1944, which was 85 days after its capture. Shipments continued into 1946 to supply the close-out force in Europe, the Allied armies of occupation in Germany, and various civilian and other needs.

Abbreviations:

P.O.L. = Petrol (gasoline) Oil Lubricants.   MT = Military Transport.   Tons (metric) = 2200 pounds.

Source:

Provided to the author by the Statistics Department, Antwerp Port Authority. Originally contained in a memorandum to the Director-General of the Port from Allied military authorities.

Appendix B:
The V-Bomb Attack on Antwerp

7 October 1944 to 30 March 1945 (175 days)

Final Summary: Official Figures from the
British Civil Defence Column

Total fall of shot:

V-1:   4,248
V-2:   1,712
Total: 5,960

Casualties:

Allied military personnel	731 killed
	1,192 injured
Civilians	3,752 killed
	6,000 injured

The first

V-2: 2200 hours on 7 October 1944
V-1: 0400 hours on 11 October 1944

The last

V-1: 0007 hours on 30 March 1945
V-2: 0845 hours on 28 March 1945

Daily average over period of 175 days:

34.06 per day
24.28 V-1s
9.78 V-2s

Average per square mile:

Greater Antwerp (65 sq. mi.)	18.67
Arrondissement of Antwerp (391 sq. mi.)	9.48

Fall of shot by months:

	V-1	V-2	Total
October	131	160	291
November	481	377	858
December	632	417	1,049
January	761	367	1,128
February	1370	256	1,626
March	873	135	1,008
Total	4,248	1,712	5,960

Highest daily totals:

V-1:   111 on 8 March 1945
V-2:   27 on 22 December 1944
Both: 120 on 8 March 1945

Casualty incidents:

Allied personnel suffered casualties in 205 incidents with an average of 3.48 killed and 9.19 injured per incident. The British suffered almost ten times as many casualties as the U.S. though the numbers of personnel were almost the same.

Casualty averages:

	Per Fall of Shot		Per Incident	
	Killed	Injured	Killed	Injured
Arrondissement	1.14	3.02	2.06	5.48
Greater Antwerp	2.93	7.67	4.93	12.89
8 Communes	2.01	4.93	2.72	6.68
Antwerp Town	10.63	27.00	13.90	35.33

Port of Antwerp:

Only 211 V-1s fell in the vital dock area.

Port fatalities:

131 dock workers killed by V-bombs

Note:

Report received by the author from Captain Cooke of the British Army in Antwerp on 25 June 1945.

Appendix C:
Personnel of the 105th Port Marine Maintenance Co.

The men of the 105th trained and worked together for a year and a half in successful pursuit of their company mission. They were a heterogeneous group with a diverse mix of geographic, ethnic, educational, occupational and cultural backgrounds, yet they became an effective, cohesive organization. Best of all, they never took the army too seriously and they knew how to have fun together. They truly were a bunch of mavericks.

Enlisted Men

George W. Adams
Julius E. Albert
Duane Albro
Powell B. Anderson
Walter E. Anderson
Wayne Ankrum
James D. Ansell
John H. Armour
Marco Balzarin
George H. Bart
Allen W. Beal
Herman G. Beier
Robert B. Bell
Frank C. Bender
Walter F. Bennett
Benninghoff
Robert R. Bertholdt
Wilson P. Bier
John E. Bobal Jr.
Joseph E. Bogar
James W. Boggs
Thornton E. Boggus
Roman G. Boguszewski
George P. Borcina
Ray Borden
Merle E. Brooks
Wilbur C. Brown
Ray W. Buehler
Gerald S. Burton
Frederick E. Butzback

Nile G. Calhoun
Onofrio Capobianco
Frank A. Carlson
Elie Cartan
Murphy E. Carter
Russell T. Casadonti
Edward L. Casselman
John A. Castagna
Stanley P. Cepauskas
Robert L. Chapman
Joseph S. Chrustuski
Vernon R. Clack
Charles E. Connor
Frank Connors Jr.
Frederick L. Crawford
Hugh E. Crum
John C. Davis
Julius A. Deason
John DeMario
Joseph DePaulo
Fred Deutscher
Alfred Ditelli
Charles E. Duttus
Guerino Divecchia
Edward A. DiVencent
Donald H. Dodds
Cyril J. Dolbeare
Joseph Domolki Jr.
Paul K. Douvros
Walter A. Dumont

John K. Eaton
Elwood Eberly
Raymond T. Edwards
Joseph C. Ekstrom
Clarence E. Elliott
Robert L. Ellison
John J. Emrich Jr.
Hubert H. Englert
Otto Fech
Sam Feder
Gilbert Feilhauer
Anthony M. Ferrulo
Andrew P. Ferski
Frank Fettig
Robert J. Fox
Robert E. Frizell
Raymond H. Fye
Richard J. Gage
John Gardiner
Joseph H. Gardner
Fernal J. Gautreaux
Martin F. Gavin
Martin J. Gaynor
Edward J. Geistlinger
Charles F. Gerlinger
William F. Gillette
Frank J. Godfrey
Donald V. Goff
Ned H. Goldin
Louis G. Good
Thomas J. Gouge
Paul A. Grady
Robert L. Gray
George V. Greene Jr.
Herschel W. Greer
David R. Gross
Paul H. Gross
Eldridge S. Hall
Richard M. Hardy
James A. Harmon
Charles G. Harrison
Harry Hartenberg
Leslie M. Haun
George N. Havens
Donald B. Henderson
Charles Henderson

Joseph L. Hermann
Walter L. Hess
Charles N. Hickman
Carl Hilding
Manuel Hinajosa
Julius E. Holifield
Spiro Horsites
Vernon Howser
Rowland C. Hubbard
Harold C. Hunter
Albert K. Hunze
Eugene W. Hussey
Joseph F. Janda
Daniel B. Jeffers
Harold E. Jenkins
Lewis W. Jernigan
Benjamin Kaplan
Michael Karpew
Chester C. Kay
Joseph T. Kelley
Glenn F. Klein
Kloetz
John Knudsen Jr.
Edward E. Krieger
John Kubasta
Edward E. Kyle
William J. LaBrie
Milton E. Lancaster
Early D. Langford
Daniel J. Lanzetta
Holmes G. Law
Peter P. Laychack
Michael J. LeDoux
John C. Leger
Joseph M. Lillis
Donald C. Lobb
James E. Loranger
William J. Lorrigan
Carl F. Lovelady
Fred G. Lynn
Augie L. Macaluso
Christopher M. MacNee
James F. Manfredi
Leo E. Marcovitz
Donald G. Mantheny
Andrew Matzelle

Joseph R. Mayer
John A. McBride
Edward D. McCord
Roy E. McKernan
Charles L. McManus
Kenneth E. McNulty
Gilbert G. Metheny
Roy J. Miceli
Arthur Michaels
Otis G. Miller
Ned E. Miller
John A. Moeller
Arthur G. Moore
Spior Moraites
Evan M. Murphy
Christopher Murphy
Myles F. Murray
William Nawalsky
Vincent Newton
George W. Nicholson
Aloysius A. Nickels
Vern M. Niemi
James R. O'Connor
Jonathan M. Ogilvie
Henry Orti
Neil Palmieri
Jewell F. Parker
Irving Parks
Wilmot S. Parlow
Mark J. Pennachio
Howard E. Perry
Thomas R. Perso
Charles M. Peterson
Harold Pfeffer
Norman N. Pfifer
Carl Phillips
Pischer
Arthur R. Pitassi
Louis J. Plank
Alfred L. Ploetz
Raymond E. Plude
Floyd Plym
Peter P. Pomarico
Steve Popin
Oscar W. Porter
William T. Powers

Preston
Oscar Price
William B. Proctor
Buddy Pugh
Kenneth Pugliese
William F. Redden
Melvin A. Reid
Reuben S. Ren
John P. Richardson
Woodrow W. Riffle
Fred W. Rimer
Albert J. Rist
John C. Robbins
Geraldo P. Roche
John W. Rogers
Ralph M. Ross
Joseph C. Rowland
James E. Ryan
Chester A. Saltsman
John L. Sands
Germano N. Santulli
Arnold A. Schippers
Thomas R. Schneck
Dale C. Schrader
Albert Schwartz
Harry D. Shanker
Charles J. Sherman
John E. Shirley
Andrew V. Skeen
Earl C. Slager
Leo V. Sliney
Edward J. Sloan
Wilbur J. Smith
George F. Smith
Joseph L. Sommerfield
Lloyd H. St. Louis
Theodore L. Stautz
Harold M. Stebhen
Fred W. Stinnett
Joseph L. Stoddard
Stanley H. Stout
Seymour Straoco
George Strick
Timothy C. Sullivan Jr.
Hayward Sutherland
Dallas Sweeney

Robert L. Swinney
Chris Talas
Robert C. Taylor
William P. Thompson
Thomas J. Thornton
Frank E. Tischer
Carl Titus
George H. Torrealba
Richard M. Toscani
Richard M. Towle
Harold L. Tschop
Raymond P. Tunila
Otto H. Unzicker
Carl I. Van Curen
Aldo Veronelli
Morris Volpe
Gordon D. Wagner
Robert S. Wallace

Arthur R. Weiss
Charles J. Werder
James D. Wharton
Arthur H. White
Lyle J. White
Roland H. White
Keith Whitlock Sr.
Neil F. Wilcox
Casper G. Wild
Calvin D. Williams
Norman Wright
Walter D. Wright

Officers

George W. Doran, Commanding Officer
Roland G. Gwynn
Edwin Jennings
Carl J. Knecht
Robert M. Rodman
William F. Savage
Roy L. Stephens Jr.

Note:

The above list includes all personnel who served in the 105th Port Marine Maintenance Co. during its existence. The total exceeds the authorized number of personnel as many men were transferred in and/or out during this period.

Bibliography

The volume of literature on World War II is prodigious and steadily growing. This is a selective list of readings which the author has found useful and meaningful.

Stephen E. Ambrose. *D-Day June 6, 1944: The Climactic Battle of World War II*. New York: Simon & Schuster, 1994.

Stephen E. Ambrose. *Citizen Soldiers*. New York: Simon & Schuster, 1997.

Gerald Astor. *A Blood-dimmed Tide: The Battle of the Bulge*. New York: Donald I. Fine, 1992.

Omar N. Bradley. *A Soldier's Story*. New York: Henry Holt, 1951.

Omar N. Bradley. *A General's Life*. New York: Simon & Schuster, 1974.

Winston S. Churchill. *The Second World War* (Six Volumes). Boston: Houghton Mifflin, 1953.

Winston S. Churchill. *Memoirs of the Second World War*. Boston: Houghton Mifflin, 1959.

Carlo D'Este. *Patton: A Genius for War*. New York: HarperCollins, 1995.

Trevor Dupuy. *Hitler's Last Gamble: The Battle of the Bulge.* New York: HarperCollins, 1994.

David Eisenhower. *Eisenhower at War 1943-45.* New York: Random House, 1986.

Dwight D. Eisenhower. *Crusade in Europe.* New York: Doubleday, 1948.

H. Essame. *Patton: A Study in Command.* New York: Charles Scribner's Sons, 1974.

James M. Gavin. *On to Berlin.* New York: Viking, 1978.

Norman Gelb. *Ike & Monty: Generals at War.* New York: William Morrow, 1994.

Doris Kearns Goodwin. *No Ordinary Times. Franklin & Eleanor Roosevelt: The Home Front in World War II.* New York: Simon & Schuster, 1994.

Louis E. Keefer. *Scholars in Foxholes.* Reston, VA: COTU Publishing, 1988.

David Kennedy. *Freedom from Fear.* New York: Oxford University Press, 1999.

Robert Leckie. *Delivered from Evil: The Saga of World War II.* New York: Harper Perennial, 1987.

Charles R. MacDonald. *A Time for Trumpets: The Untold Story of the Battle of the Bulge.* New York: William Morrow, 1985.

Williamson Murray & Allan R. Millett. *A War to Be Won: Fighting the Second World War.* Cambridge, MA: Harvard University Press, 2000.

J.L. Moulton. *Battle for Antwerp.* London: Ian Allan Ltd, 1978

Michael J. Neufeld. *The Rocket and the Reich.* New York: The Free Press, 1995.

Richard Overy. *Why the Allies Won.* New York: W.W. Norton, 1995.

William C. Pagonis. *Leadership in a Combat Zone.* Harvard Business Review, December 2001.

Cornelius Ryan. *A Bridge Too Far.* New York: Simon & Schuster, 1974.

Studs Terkel. *"The Good War."* New York: Pantheon, 1984.

Russell F. Weigley. *Eisenhower's Lieutenants.* Bloomington: Indiana University Press, 1990.

Endnotes

1. Doris Kearns Goodwin. *No Ordinary Times. Franklin & Eleanor Roosevelt: The Home Front in World War II.* New York: Simon & Schuster, 1994.

2. Dwight D. Eisenhower. *Crusade in Europe.* New York: Doubleday, 1948, p. 235.

3. William C. Pagonis. *Leadership in a Combat Zone,* Harvard Business Review, December 2001, p. 114.

4. Goodwin. *No Ordinary Times,* p. 391.

5. S.L.A. Marshall. *Men Against Fire: The Problem of Combat Command in Future War:* Apollo Edition, New York: Morrow, 1966, pp. 50-60.

6. British Civil Defence Column report, author's file.

7. David M. Kennedy. *Freedom from Fear.* New York: Oxford University Press, 1999, p.635.

8. Louis E. Keefer. *Scholars in Foxholes.* Reston, Va: COTU Publishing, 1988, jacket copy.

9. Keefer. Scholars in Foxholes, p. 154.

10. Letter from the Adjutant General of the War Department dated 1 March 1944. Subject: Constitution and Activation of Certain Transportation Corps Units.

11. Omar N. Bradley. *A General's Life*. New York: Simon & Schuster, 1983, p.112.

12. Author's personal correspondence.

13. J.L. Moulton. *Battle for Antwerp*. London: Ian Allan Ltd., 1978, p. 62.

14. David M. Kennedy. *Freedom from Fear*, p. 733.

15. Winston S. Churchill, *Memoirs of the Second World War*. Boston: Houghton Mifflin, 1959.

16. Adapted from Russell F. Weigley. *Eisenhower's Lieutenants*. Bloomington: Indiana University Press, 1981; Winston S. Churchill. *Memoirs of the Second World War*. Boston: Houghton Mifflin, 1959; The Port of Antwerp Website; and the author's personal observations.

17. Rudi Velthuis, et al. *v2rocket.com* (Website), p.2

18. Kennedy. *Freedom from Fear*, p.736.

19. David Eisenhower. *Eisenhower at War*. New York: Random House, 1986, p.434-4..

20. Weigley. *Eisenhower's Lieutenants*. P.350.

21. Moulton. *Battle for Antwerp*. p. 82.

22. Ibid, p.94

23. Ibid, p. 95

24. Williamson Murray & Allan Millett. *A War to Be Won: Fighting the Second World War.* Cambridge, Mass: Harvard University Press, 2000. p. 458.

25. Moulton. *Battle for Antwerp*, p. 6.

26. James M. Gavin. *On to Berlin.* New York: Viking, 1978. p. 139.

27. Moulton. *Battle for Antwerp*, p.182

28. Murray & Millett. *A War to Be Won.* P.434-440.

29. David Eisenhower. *Eisenhower at War*, p-484-488.

30. Moulton. *Battle for Antwerp*, p. 182-6.

31. Antwerp Port Authority archives, memo to the Director-General.

32. Moulton. *Battle for Antwerp*, p. 185.

33. Collie Small. *How Antwerp Was Saved.* Saturday Evening Post, 21 July 1945, p. 19, 82.

34. Michael J. Neufeld. *The Rocket and the Reich.* New York: The Free Press, 1995, p. 147.

35. Ibid, p. 274.

36. Kennedy. *Freedom from Fear.* P. 734.

37. Neufeld. *The Rocket and the Reich*, p. 281-2.

38. Stephen E. Ambrose. *D-Day June 6, 1944: The Climactic Battle of World War II.* New York: Simon & Schuster, 1994, p. 482.

39. Norman Gelb. *Ike & Monty: Generals at War.* New York: William Morrow, 1994, p. 323.

40. Rudi Velthuis. *v2rocket.com*, p. 22.

41. Neufeld. *The Rocket and the Reich*, p. 249.

42. Rudi Velthuis. *v2rocket.com*, p. 12.

43. Moulton. Battle for Antwerp, p. 230.

44. Velthuis. *V2rocket.com*, p.22.

45. Jared Diamond. *Keeping Panic at Bay*, New York Times, October 21, 2001, page 15.

46. Velthuis, *v2rocket.com*, p. 9.

47. British Civil Defence Column report, author's file.

48. Collie Small. *How Antwerp Was Saved*, p. 82.

49. Russell F. Weigley. *Eisenhower's Lieutenants*, Bloomington: Indiana University Press, 1981, p. 605.

50. Kennedy, *Freedom from Fear*, p. 739

51. Carlo D'Este. *Patton: A Genius for War.* New York: HarperCollins, 1995, p. 676.

52. Author's personal correspondence.

53. Author's personal correspondence.

54. Author's personal correspondence.

Index

Notes

Notes

Notes

Notes

Notes

The ASTPers at the 105th company reunion in 1994: (L to R) Louis Good, Ray Buehler, Roy McKernan and the author.

The surviving mavericks of the 105th at a company reunion on the 50th anniversary of the company's founding. (Front L to R) Otto Unzicker; Herschel Greer; the author; Joe Mayer; Julius Albert, Augie Macaluso. (Rear L to R) Verne Niemi, Roy McKernan, Ray Buehler, Fred Crawford, George Greene, Louis Good, Seymour Strauch, Frank Carlson, Mark Pennachio, Chester Kay, Al Ploetz, Bob Bell.